ISLAMIC FINANCE IN THE CIS COUNTRIES

ALMIRA Z. NAGIMOVA

ACADEMUS
Publishing

Academus Publishing
2021

Academus Publishing, Inc.

1999 S, Bascom Avenue, Suite 700 Campbell CA 95008
Website: www.academuspublishing.com
E-mail: info@academuspub.com

The research is funded by RFBR, project number 19-310-60002
"Islamic Finance in the post-Soviet space: challenges and opportunities
for investment growth in the CIS coutries".

The right of Almira Z. Nagimova, PhD in Economics, senior research associate
at the Institute of International Relations of Kazan (Volga) Federal University
is identified as author of this work.

For e-mail correspondence: nagimova_almira@mail.ru

ISBN 10: 1 4946 0020 X
ISBN 13: 978 1 4946 0020 4
DOI 10.31519/0021-8

Over the past decades, Islamic Finance has expanded its presence to many countries, including the former Soviet Union. It is not surprising that its expansion has become a subject of great interest to scholars, politicians, practitioners, and the general public. How big is the market for Islamic Finance in the post-Soviet region? Who are the key market players? What are their investment strategies on this territory? Finally, what are the limits for the development of the Islamic Finance industry in the CIS countries? This book attempts to find the answers to these questions by examining a broad empirical base of more than 1,000 deals from 1991 to 2020, as well as using a sociological approach. Another attempt has been made to assess the total volume of Islamic capital and determine the problems and prospects of this market in the CIS countries.

The book will be of interest to the management of banks, investment companies, funds, ministries, as well as anyone interested in the world economy, international relations and the religious factor in the economy of post-Soviet countries.

INTRODUCTION

Almost 30 years have passed since the dissolution of the Soviet Union and the collapse of the Communist regime. Since then, basing on its historical roots, Islam has once again begun to occupy the space opening in the ideological field of the post-Soviet states. Over these years Islam in the CIS countries has evidently tended to gradually expand: new mosques and madrassas were opened, an increasing number of believers began to attend Friday prayers and observe fasting in the Holy month of Ramadan. However, at the same time, the opposite process took place: the authorities of the CIS countries viewed the growth of religious identity of the population as a threat to public order and political stability. Strict observance of religious norms has become increasingly seen as a sign of radicalization. An intolerant prejudice that religion should be restricted still prevails in the socio-political discourse. However, it would be naive to believe that the Muslim population of this territory (which is more than 90 mln people) can be fenced off from the ideas that were developed during a long history of uninterrupted Islamic traditions. Islamic Finance understood in this study as a set of financial institutions and instruments that comply with Shariah (Islamic law) is a striking example of this. In his remarkable book "No god but God", R. Aslan, an American scholar of Iranian origin, summarizes Shariah as "a set of rules, a code of conduct that forever transformed Islam from a religion into a way of life covering all spheres of its activity" (Aslan, 2019). According to another scholar, B. Lewis, in its socio-political aspect Shariah is "not only a normative set of laws, but also a model of behavior, an ideal to which individuals and society as a whole should strive" (Lewis, 2017).

However, before we turn to Islamic Finance, we will give a brief overview of the history and origins of the issue relying on the works of the above-mentioned historians. After studying the history of religion, R. Aslan came to the conclusion that the prophet Muhammad "called for social reforms long before he established a new religion. Prior to preaching monotheism he already demanded economic justice". In Muhammad's sermons, "the mistreatment and exploitation of the weak and defenseless were condemned in the strongest possible terms.

He encouraged to suppress false contracts and the practice of usury that led to poor people being enslaved". Thus, during his lifetime, the prophet Muhammad "categorically outlawed usury, the abuse of which was one of the main claims to the religious and economic system" of the society of that era. This decision was intended to soften the "gap between the incredibly rich and the extraordinarily poor". This example clearly demonstrates how many parallels arise between the times when, according to R. Aslan "the unprotected masses of the population were exploited to maintain the welfare and power of the elite", and modernity. The problems of social injustice and uneven distribution of wealth are still relevant today. Therefore, it is not surprising that the ideas of Islamic Economics and Finance receive a wide response in the hearts of our contemporaries. However, their full conceptualization in the framework of special theory will take a long time, and meanwhile in the flourishing of Islamic civilization, according to B. Lewis (2017), "money changers were an integral part of any Muslim market", and by the IX century they "turned into big bankers". History offers many examples of medieval banks in the Middle East with an extensive network of branches and a "complex system of checks". Merchants of that time had Bank accounts and "insisted on paying in cheques instead of cash". The historian writes that at that time "some schools of thought believed that a reasonable interest rate was not considered usury", but still, it was precisely because of the ban on usury that Muslim bankers were rather few in numbers. Since then, the Islamic world has experienced periods of prosperity and decline, Ottoman rule and European occupation, but a solution was not found until the twentieth century. In the 1970s, the first commercial Islamic Bank, Dubai Islamic Bank, opened in the UAE, the Islamic Development Bank in Saudi Arabia, and many similar private and public institutions in Kuwait, Bahrain, Malaysia, Sudan, and Egypt. The conceptual framework of Islamic financial structures are the Islamic financial principles which presuppose:

- *first*, the prohibition of usury, understood as excessive and unjustified compensation for transactions (*riba*);
- *second*, the prohibition on uncertainty, understood as the opacity, ambiguity and asymmetry of information in transactions (*gharar*);
- *third*, the exclusion of financing and dealing in sinful activities for the production and sale of alcohol, tobacco, pork, weapons, entertainment, gambling, etc. (*haram*);
- *fourth*, risk-sharing between the owner of capital and the entrepreneur;

4

- *fifth*, the materiality of the transaction, which is expressed in direct or indirect connection with real assets;
- *sixth*, justice, understood as the absence of exploitation of one party of the transaction by the other party (Gait, and Worthington, 2007).

Today, the market of Islamic Finance is dominated by seven countries: Iran (with a market share of 30% of the world), Saudi Arabia (24%), Malaysia (11%), the United Arab Emirates (10%), Qatar (6%), Kuwait (5%) and Bahrain (4%). In one form or another, represented in more than 60 countries, the total assets of Islamic Finance exceed $2trln. Being criticized for their conservatism, Islamic banks, however, survived the global financial crisis of 2007–2008 with less losses (Hasan, and Dridi, 2010). Over the past decade, even taking into account the crisis, the Islamic financial sector has seen an annual growth rate of 10–12%. At the same time, the conventional financial system based on interest rates added 1–2% per year. Islamic Finance is not only about Islamic banks, but also funds, insurance, leasing, and microfinance companies. Islamic financial services can also be provided through Islamic windows[1] within conventional banks. Sukuk[2], the Islamic bond market, has become an important segment of the global financial market, too. The reasons for the success of Islamic Finance in the world are too numerous and complex to reveal them in detail here. But researchers name Turkey, as well as densely populated Indonesia and Muslim countries in Africa, as the drivers of market growth in the long term. However, the CIS countries have not been left out of this incredibly successful project. Since the young post-Soviet states gained sovereignty, the history of Islamic Finance has been constantly developing here as well. This book represents an attempt to identify the logic whereby Islamic Finance is rooted in the economic practices of the CIS countries.

---

[1] Islamic window is a separate branch or department that operates within a conventional Bank and provides products and services in accordance with Islamic financial principles. The accounts and financial resources of the conventional Bank and the Islamic window should not be 'mixed'. The Islamic window allows conventional banks to expand the portfolio of banking products offered to businesses and the public without major additional investments, and at least reach customers who adhere to the norms of Islam.

[2] Sukuk is understood as Islamic bonds that represent the holder's right to a certain share of the profit generated by the asset over a certain period of time until maturity.

LITERATURE REVIEW

To date, the topic of Islamic Finance is represented by a large body of works some of which give insights into the complexity and versatility of this phenomenon and are relevant for the current study. Thus, I. Warde (2000) giving a deep analysis of Islamic Finance makes an important conclusion for all subsequent researchers: "Islamic Finance is not a monolithic, unchanging and somewhat fossilized" phenomenon, but rather reflects the diversity of Islam in different continents. He emphasizes that Islamic Finance "cannot be captured without full understanding of religion and finance, but also of history, politics, economics, business, and culture". Moreover, according to Warde, "such an economic perspective misses the whole point of religiously-motivated behavior", so "appreciating the complexity of human motivations" in the process of choosing financial services is of crucial importance when analyzing this phenomenon.

In another work employing the data of 2008—2009 for their empirical research of the effects of the global crisis on Islamic and conventional banks Hasan and Dridi (2010) from International Monetary Fund have shown that Islamic banks are more resistant to financial crises than conventional ones. This paper emphasizes that "while conventional intermediation is largely debt-based and allows for risk transfer, Islamic intermediation, in contrast, is asset-based, and centers on risk sharing". Probably it was this work that sparked a new wave of quantitative research on Islamic Finance, as well as public and media interest in this topic.

"Islamic Finance in Europe" carried out by a team of economists of the European Central Bank (Mauro, etc., 2013) presents a regional study on the role of Islamic Finance in the Western economy. Interest in this topic was caused primarily by "the financial crisis and the resulting call for building a more stable and secure financial system" in Europe.

With regard to the post-Soviet area, A. Wolters (2013) has shown that Islamic Finance "serves as a phenomenon that is well suited to inform us about the relation between religion and economy, and state and religion in the region". British scientist D. Hoggarth (2016) investigated Islamic Finance in the context of postcolonial construction of peace in Central Asia and Russia and came to the conclusion that the conventional and Islamic banking systems "are in fact closely entwined, existing as parts of a larger financial system, rather than one being an alternative to the other". Continuing Hoggarth's line of reasoning, it can be argued that this understanding contradicts the "binary interpretation" of Islamic Finance as a "clash of civilizations", which leads to a perception of Islamic Finance as "an anti-modern system, rather than as an evolving construct". In this work, Hoggarth draws a significant conclusion: "Any failure to explore the diversity within Islam compromises our understanding of what it means to self-identify with the religion in a place", so it can become a serious obstacle in the study of attitudes to Islamic Finance in post-Soviet society. The general conclusion of this work is that the issue of Islamic Finance in the CIS countries is "a complex and has been poorly understood" and needs further conceptualization.

As for CIS research, in this area, it has had both a lower capacity and lack of evidence base as compared to the international science. Local religious traditions and the complexity of the environment in which Islamic financial organizations are forced to exist on this territory are often left out of the research context. In addition, local research lacks interdisciplinary approaches giving an opportunity to look at this very complex phenomenon located at the intersection of finance, culture, traditions, psychology and religious beliefs from different angles. Thus, in (Aliyev, 2012) a thesis that Islamic Finance "has never been seen as a purely financial institution", but "has always been partially political" tends to be hasty and not supported by scientific evidence. The same conviction was expressed by experts of the Skolkovo (2018) Institute for Emerging Market Studies in their report "The Islamic economy — The Fastest Growing Large Economy. Eurasian focus": they believe that the only chance to develop for the Islamic economy in Eurasia lies within the framework of the Muslim food industry and fashion (Halal industry), which should stimulate further demand for Islamic financial products. Such a conclusion has probably come as a result of an untenable analysis of the market and its growth drivers. Meanwhile, some of Aliyev's (2012) observations are relevant: for example, he defines politicians' suspicions of Islamic Finance as "hidden Islamophobia" based on the perceived threat posed by any type of Islamic activity against secular nationalism and the existing authoritarian regimes in the CIS.

Another example can be found in (Bekkin, 2010) where the author of the most cited work on Islamic Finance in the Russian language argues that "the main obstacle to Islamic Finance in Russia" is a low level of business ethics among businesspeople and ordinary consumers of financial services. This conclusion, especially in the light of our findings

7

(Chapter 7), can hardly be seen as fair or unbiased. Nevertheless, it is this scholar who should be commended for laying the foundations of traditions in the study of Islamic Finance in the CIS. In the 2000s, a lot of new young researchers showed interest in studying Islamic Finance: E. Biryukov, M. Kalimullina, I. Zaripov, M. Yandiyev, and others. Many new papers have been published by scholars from universities in Tatarstan, Bashkortostan, Chechnya, and Dagestan. In all these works, though, the range of issues discussed remained mainly within the general approaches outlined by R. Bekkin, and so far no original approaches to the study of Islamic Finance have been offered. Thus, despite an increasing number of sources allowing to make new discoveries and generalizations, we can still find statements of the following type: "the social component of the philosophy of Islamic Finance affects the entire state system", "Islam prohibits bank interest, simply appealing to God, without explaining the economic side of the matter", etc. However, it should be recognized that a number of CIS scholars have made a great contribution to research in this area. Thus, Chokaev (2015) makes an important observation: most Islamic banks do not operate in developed countries, where "existing legislative and judicial systems provide good protection of private property, protection of investors' rights, and guarantee the fulfillment of contracts", but in developing countries, where "these elements are still weak". The author concludes that "in order to achieve maximum efficiency of the Islamic banking system, it is necessary to create favorable conditions for the use of equity participation instruments".

In 2013, the modest author published one of her first works (Nagimova, 2013) which attempts to estimate the volume of Arab investment in Russia. The following series of articles explores mutual investment between the Gulf States and the CIS countries from different perspectives, using a transactional approach to the economy within the framework of R. Coase's neo-institutional theory. One of the latest publications (Nagimova, 2020), gives a detailed review of mergers and acquisitions (M&A) and attempts to determine the size of Arab investments in the energy, road, port, airport, warehouse, social and IT infrastructure of Russia, and also identifies problems of attracting Arab capital to the country.

In Kalimullina (2010a) survey of more than 1,000 respondents found that 80% of them are ready to become clients of Islamic banks. a new observation was made: the presence of religious education correlates with the refusal to "interact with conventional financial organizations". The author concludes that the factors hindering the development of Islamic financial products include the low level of education and enlightenment, primarily religious. "To make Islamic financial products attractive, we need to provide information support for various initiatives in this area and develop educational programs. But real projects related to Islamic Finance in Russia should be aimed at solving the most urgent problems for people: education, mortgages for young families, investments in small and medium-sized businesses on fair terms".

CHAPTER 1.
KAZAKHSTAN

In early 2010, in his message to the people of Kazakhstan, the first President of the country, N. Nazarbayev, stated that by the year 2020 the Republic is to become "a regional center of Islamic banking in the CIS and Central Asia and enter the top ten financial centers of the world"[1]. The government supported the enthusiasm of the head of state and planned to fund a tenth of the economy of Kazakhstan by 2020 using Islamic Finance[2]. An example was Malaysia, where the share of Islamic banks in the economy has nearly reached 30%[3]. As the British researcher D. Hoggarth (2016) put it in her work "The rise of Islamic finance: post-colonial market-building in Central Asia and Russia": "the Kazakh government is looking eastwards for strategic concepts". Indeed, some important historical parallels can be drawn here: in the aftermath of the 1985–1986 recession, the Malaysian government set a fundamentally new course of economic development based on reduced public spending, partial privatization, progressive deregulation, and financial market liberalization. The latter, as well as the strong initiative of the Malaysian government in the realization of the Financial Sector Master Plan, presented in 2001 by the Central Bank, contributed to the rapid growth of Islamic Finance in the country. It is symbolic that the same experts who worked on similar laws in Malaysia were invited to make changes on Islamic Finance in Kazakhstan's legislation. However, despite this nuance, by the beginning of 2020, the share of Islamic Finance in the economy of Kazakhstan is estimated at less than 0.2%. Let's try to understand why the Kazakh authorities failed to achieve this goal over the past decades. However, before proceeding to the analysis and identifying limiting factors, we will agree that the development of Islamic Finance will not be taken out of the context of social, economic and political changes in the country.

---

[1] https://www.akorda.kz/ru/addresses/addresses_of_president/poslanie-prezidenta-respubliki-kazakhstan-n-a-nazarbaeva-narodu-kazakhstana-29-yanvarya-2010-goda_1340624693

[2] https://tengrinews.kz/news/2020-godu-dolya-islamskih-finansov-ekonomike-rk-dostignet-10-67196/

[3] Malaysia ranks 3rd in the world (after Iran and Saudi Arabia) in terms of Islamic financial assets. In addition, Malaysia is a pioneer and permanent leader in issuing sukuk, Islamic bonds (IFSB, 2018).

Thus, having gained independence in 1991, Kazakhstan, like most of the CIS countries, was in economic decline for almost a whole decade: for example, the country's GDP (in current prices) for 1991–1998 decreased by 11%. This was both a consequence of the negative situation on the commodity markets (the price of Brent crude oil for the same period did not exceed $25 per barrel), and the strong dependence of Kazakhstan on the economic position of Russia which was the country's main trade and geopolitical partner at that time. As we can see from Fig.1.1, after a 5-year recession in 1991–1995, the economy of Kazakhstan grew slightly in 1996–1997, but in 1998 it shrank again due to the fall in oil prices and the economic crisis of 1998. After recovering by 2.7% In 1999, the annual economic growth in 2000–2006 averaged 10%, while in 2001 it showed a record value of 13.5%. Despite rapid development of many sectors of the economy, it is evident that the boom was provided by the oil and gas sector[1]. From 1998 to 2007, the price of Brent crude oil increased by more than 5 times, and Kazakhstan's GDP over the same period added an average of 9% annually. However, heavy dependence on the same commodity sector caused an economic downturn in Kazakhstan after the global financial crisis of 2007–2008 and a new cycle of falling oil prices: in 2009, the economic growth slowed to 1.8%. Due to improved conditions in the oil market in 2010–2011, the Kazakh economy recovered and showed more than 7% growth, but never again did the GDP growth rate reach 10%, as it was during the years of the 'oil prosperity'. Moreover, in 2015–2016, the economic growth slowed again to 1.1–1.2%, which was due to falling energy prices and the implementation of geopolitical risks against the country's key trade and economic partner, Russia[2]. In addition, in 2009 and 2014, the Kazakh authorities twice devalued the national currency, tenge, and in 2015, following the example of Russia, the country switched to a floating exchange rate. In addition, in 2009 and 2014, the Kazakh authorities twice devalued the national currency tenge, and in 2015, following the example of Russia, the country switched to a floating exchange rate. In 2017–2018, the recovery in commodity prices and large foreign investments in the oil and gas investment projects contributed to economic growth of 4.1% per year.

---

[1] According to The World Factbook, Kazakhstan is ranked 9th in crude oil exports and 17th in natural gas exports in the world.

[2] In 2014, Western countries introduce the 1st package of anti-Russian sanctions which, in addition to the sanctions list of top officials, includes restrictions on access to capital markets and technologies for the mining companies.

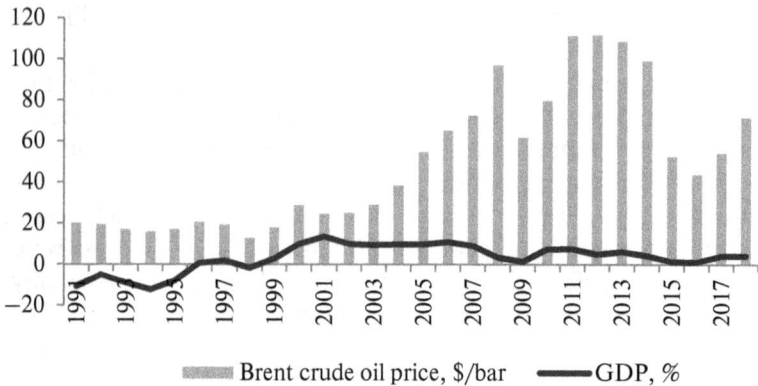

Fig. 1.1. Dynamics of Kazakhstan's GDP and Brent crude oil
prices growth for the period from 1991 to 2018
Source: compiled from EIU Data Services[1]

Thus, two cycles of falling world oil prices and economic crises have shown the illusory nature of not only the 'Kazakh economic miracle', but even economic stability in the country. Moreover, the economic turmoil in Kazakhstan was accompanied by a full-scale crisis in the banking sector caused by the generation of 'toxic' assets[2]. This, in turn, was a consequence of the local banks' access to cheap funding in West and the weakening of standards for assessing the reliability of borrowers. Then Kazakh banks were 'saved' at the expense of foreign investors and the state. In general, it became clear that the entire financial system of the country, tied to Western markets, is vulnerable and needs a large-scale structural reforms.

Returning to Islamic Finance, it should be noted that before the global financial crisis they were viewed with irony, sometimes even with fear[3], but after its onset the Kazakhstanis' attitude to this topic has changed. From a practical point of view, it was clear that in order to achieve sustainable and long-term growth the country needed to diversify its economy and sources of financing, and from an ideological point of view, there was a need for a multi-vector strategy that reduces economic dependence on one direction only. In addition, according to D. Hoggarth (2016), the Islamic financial project for Kazakhstan

---

[1] https://eiu.bvdep.com
[2] This includes loans with overdue debts (Non-Performing Loans) over 90 days.
[3] The latter is caused by a new wave of Islamophobia in the West in the early 2000s (read more about the history and current state of the issue, for example (Gottschalk, and Greenberg, 2008)).

"images of the state's religious tolerance and diversity <...> by providing growth without radical democratic reform".

Moving chronologically, we note that in 2007 a special working group on Islamic Finance is created under the "Association of financiers of Kazakhstan" with attraction of a grant from the Islamic Development Bank and the experience of international experts. In 2008, the Arab fund Alnair Capital[1].becomes the majority shareholder of the distressed Kazkommertsbank. 2009 is the year of creating the 'Association for the Development of Islamic Finance' which A. Wolters (2013) calls "a clear lobby group" responsible for facilitating "the reform of legislation and work on behalf of its members' interests". In the same year, 2009, the 1st package of laws on Islamic Finance is adopted[2], and a 2-year roadmap for the development of Islamic Finance is approved. In 2012, this roadmap is expanded to 41 points and approved for the period until 2020. At the same time, in 2012, the Department of Islamic Finance is opened at the National Bank of Kazakhstan. As we can see, in many ways, it was the global financial crisis of 2007–2008 that catalyzed the growth of interest in Islamic Finance. In the following years, not only an institutional development of the industry takes place, but also an extensive practice of attracting Islamic capital in various areas. In using Islamic Finance, "Kazakhstan is placing itself in a category with other successful states that have gone on to develop strong Islamic financial markets, such as Malaysia and Bahrain" (Hoggarth, 2016). Moreover, according to Hoggarth, Islamic Finance helps to strengthen the brand of Kazakhstan in some unexpected ways: first, it allows us to "assert the departure from a Soviet past defined by corruption, a weak economic structure and lack of religious tolerance", and second, "reconnects Kazakhstan to its pre-Soviet identity", but "rather than creating the image of a 'backward-facing' society, it simultaneously projects a desire to be a dynamic market leader", of the modern economy.

We have collected and analyzed a broad empirical base consisting of more than 250 deals involving Islamic capital in Kazakhstan for the period from 1991 to 2020. The initial source for us was Bureau van Dijk's ZEPHYR and ORBIS databases[3], then the data was significantly expanded by content analysis

---

[1] The Fund is owned by a banker and Sheikh Abu Dhabi Tahnoon bin Zayed Al Nahyan, one of the 30 children of the first President of the UAE. It is known that at the end of 2015 Kazkommertsbank again comes under the control of a local businessman K. Rakishev.

[2] Referred to the Law No. 133-IV of February 12, 2009 'On Amendments and Additions to Certain Legislative Acts of the Republic of Kazakhstan on the Organization of Activities of Islamic Banks and Organizations of Islamic financing'.

[3] https://www.bvdinfo.com/en-gb

of open media sources. However, for deeper understanding and generalization, these data were insufficient, so based on the identified deals, we analyzed an array of corporate information (press releases, presentations, annual reports, interviews with management, etc.) related to them.

This approach allowed us to discover many patterns. Thus, we identified the most active Islamic investors in this country, classified them, and tried to reveal the logic of their decisions, which ultimately allowed us to determine the specifics of their investment strategies in this country. In addition, we assessed the total volume of Islamic capital in the economy of Kazakhstan and the factors limiting their qualitative and quantitative growth.

ISLAMIC DEVELOPMENT BANK GROUP

In 1995 Kazakhstan, after other CIS countries, becomes a member of the Organization of Islamic cooperation (OIC), the second largest international institution after the United Nations in terms of the number of participating countries and their population. In 2017, within the framework of this organization, Kazakhstan hosts the OIC Summit on Science and Technology, and in 2011 it initiates the *Islamic Organization for Food Security*. More than 30 member countries of the OIC become members of the latter, and its headquarters are opened in Nur-Sultan (until 2019 — Astana). In recent years, Kazakhstan has positioned itself as a food hub and center for planning agro-industrial policy in the OIC, so in 2019, in order to facilitate commodity flows in the Islamic world, N. Nazarbayev initiates a new project: Islamic Infrastructure Integration. However, while the OIC is essentially a political institution, the Islamic Development Bank (IDB) group is a financial institution that supports projects of the OIC members. The mission of the IDB is socio-economic development of the participating countries, and one of the six areas of activity is the development of the Islamic Finance industry (IDB, 2020). Therefore, it is quite logical that this development Bank provides capital to its members in accordance with Islamic financial principles, while using special Shariah standards: murabaha, istisna, ijarah and others.

The share of Kazakhstan in the subscribed capital of the IDB equals 0.11%, the amount contributed to the capital is $6 mln. In 1997, with the purpose of administering projects in Central Asia and Eastern Europe a regional office of the IDB is opened in Almaty. Like other similar development institutions, the IDB offers a number of grants to provide technical assistance to participating countries, co-finances important

14

infrastructure projects, supports the development of farming, affordable medical and educational services, etc.

Our analysis, which covered about 90 transactions financed by the IDB in Kazakhstan (Appendix B), showed that most of the capital was directed to the agricultural sector (more than $600 mln), most of which came from the Islamic trade financing of wheat supplies. This is probably being implemented within the framework of the above-mentioned project of the Islamic Food Security Organization.

The IDB allocated $300 mln to the transport infrastructure sector of Kazakhstan, including $100 mln for the construction of the 66-kilometer *Big Almaty Ring Road* (BAKAD), and $170 mln (with a profit rate of 5.1% and a maturity of 20 years) for the reconstruction of the 58-kilometer *Border of South Kazakhstan region–Taraz Road*. Both sections are key segments of the Western Europe–Western China transit corridor, the construction of which will contribute to the growth of world trade and employment. Thus, according to the European Bank for Reconstruction and Development, up to 1,700 people, 90% of which are local residents, will be involved in the construction of the highway. BAKAD is the first public-private partnership project of this kind in the whole of Central Asia and the first significant project outside the oil and gas sector in Kazakhstan. The project is implemented by a consortium of Turkish-Korean companies that have a high reputation and experience in implementing similar projects around the world. The project implementation period finishes in 2023. Besides the IDB, the project is invested by other development institutions such as the World Bank, the Asian Development Bank and the European Bank for Reconstruction and Development. a sum of more than $150 mln has been invested by the IDB in water supply projects in rural areas of Kazakhstan. In addition, using Islamic microfinance, the Bank has invested more than $40 mln in the development of farming through intermediaries: state-owned KazAgroFinance and private Nurbank. We were able to find out that the former, in its turn, financed about 1,000 farms according to the Shariah standard murabaha[1], and the latter not only allocated these funds, but also attracted additional $5 mln from the IDB's subsidiary, the Islamic Corporation for the Insurance of Investment and Export Credit (ICIEC), for the purpose of insuring

---

[1] Murabaha is one of the most widespread types of Islamic Finance consisting in the purchase of a product by a financial institution at the request of the client and the subsequent resale of this product to the client by installments with a pre-agreed and constant margin.

and export financing of trade and investment transactions of Kazakh companies in ICIEC member countries.

In 2008 the IDB provided technical assistance to the development of legislation on Islamic Finance, the institutional development of the above-mentioned Islamic Food Security Organization ($308,600 in 2014), and the creation of a master plan for the development of Islamic Finance within the framework of the Astana International Financial Center ($270,000 in 2018).

As for the financial sector, before the global crisis of 2007–2008, the main recipient of capital from the IDB among Kazakhstan's banks was BTA Bank (in 2003, the Bank received $50 mln, in 2006 — $200 mln, in 2007 — $50 mln of the Islamic capital), however after its onset in 2007, the financing was received by Halyk Bank and the above-mentioned Kazkommertsbank with the formulation "to provide access to longer term funds" ($50 mln each). It is logical that all the funds from the IDB are not only attracted, but also distributed among the Bank clients according to the Islamic Finance principles. So, according to the news sources, in 2019, the state Entrepreneurship Development Fund Dam attracted $40 mln from a subsidiary of the IDB — the Islamic Corporation for the Development of the Private Sector (ICD) with plans to invest the capital in small and medium-sized businesses through intermediaries — the Islamic Bank Al-Hilal, the Islamic leasing company KIC Leasing and the state DBK-Leasing. These loans were granted to entrepreneurs under the murabaha standard for a 7-year period, the remuneration amount was 14%, which was the best offer available at that time[1].

Of particular interest are the IDB's equity capital financing deals: for example, in 2012 the IDB invested $10 mln in the capital of Zaman Bank, and in 2013 the same amount was allocated to the capital of KIC Leasing (Kazakhstan leasing (ijarah) company). Both companies currently offer financing based on the Islamic principles. More details about them will be highlighted below.

So, the IDB is currently one of the largest Islamic investors in the economy of Kazakhstan. This international development institute has financed about 90 projects in the country for a total of $1.5 bln (excluding transactions of subsidiaries of the IDB). This is the second result, both in terms of the total number and volume of deals in the entire post-Soviet area, after Uzbekistan, where the Bank invested almost $2 bln. The average size of a single transaction in this country, therefore, is almost $17 mln (Appendix B).

---

[1] https://kursiv.kz/news/finansy/2019-01/damu-voznagrazhdenie-po-islamskim-zaymam-dlya-biznesa-sostavit-14-godovykh

ISLAMIC BANKS

In the early 1990s, there were two private Islamic banks operating on the Kazakh market — *Al-Baraka* owned by a Saudi billionaire Saleh Abdullah Kamal and *LARIBA Bank* owned by an American banker of Egyptian origin known in the world as the 'father of Islamic banking in North America', Dr. Yahia Abdul Rahman. A. Wolters (2016) specifies that the decision to open Al-Baraka was made by the Council of Ministers of the KSSR in 1990. Both banks were established as joint ventures with the government of Kazakhstan but did not last long. The first Bank was sold to LUKOIL-Kazakhstan after 5 years of existence (now it is a conventional Kaspi Bank, owned by V. Kim and others), while the second Bank was reorganized and later renamed AsiaCredit Bank which also provides conventional financing services today. Besides, in 1997 the Government of Saudi Arabia creates the *Saudi Investment Company* in Kazakhstan with a capital of $50 mln, though there is no available information about the transactions of this company. This period can be considered the first wave of private Islamic capital in the Kazakhstan market.

The second wave of Islamic investment began in the mid-2000s. At that time, conventional Kazakh banks attracted the first syndicated financing from Islamic capital markets: e.g. Alliance Bank received $150 mln, and BTA Bank received $250 mln. The latter deal in 2007 was recognized by Islamic Finance News as the 'Deal of the Year'. The Bank attracted financing for 2 years with a profit margin of 0.5% according to the Islamic financial standard of wakala[1]. 14 investors from Malaysia and the Middle East participated in the syndicate. The deal was indeed successful as the Bank's initial request for $150 mln was increased to $250 mln. The consultants of the deal were Islamic banks: Abu Dhabi Islamic Bank and others. The Bank used the raised funds for Islamic trade finance of its clients' operations. In the same 2007, following this successful transaction, BTA Bank and Emirates Islamic Bank announced the creation of the first Islamic Bank in Kazakhstan. a year later, in 2008, a similar intention and investment of $100–150 mln was announced by Qatar Islamic Bank. In 2009, Singapore Islamic Bank of Asia also announced its desire to work in Kazakhstan. However, *the first Islamic Bank Al Hilal* with an authorized capital of more than $40 mln opened in 2010, only after the Government of Kazakhstan adopted the 1st package of laws on Islamic Finance. The management of this Bank

---

[1] Wakala is an agency agreement under which an agent (wakeel) undertakes to manage the asset given to him in exchange for a certain reward (a lump sum or a share of the invested amount).

then announced ambitious investments in the economy of Kazakhstan in the amount of $1 bln, of which $200–250 mln was planned to be invested in the first year of the Bank's operation. For a young Emirati Bank at that time, this was the first experience of foreign expansion[1]. By 2014, the Bank already had offices in Almaty, Astana and Shymkent. In Kazakhstan, Al Hilal initially focused on the corporate sector and served wealthy clients, but then it began to develop its retail business: in 2017, the Bank issued Islamic debit cards for the first time, and in 2018, together with the state-owned Housing construction saving bank of Kazakhstan, it introduced Islamic mortgages to the retail market. It is noteworthy that in its home market, in the UAE, Al Hilal successfully developed both directions, and the Kazakh business brought no more than 2.5% of revenue from Islamic financial operations. But in 2019, the Bank, already a member of the Abu Dhabi Commercial Bank Group, announced a new strategy for transformation into a digital financial platform for retail clients[2]. According to the consolidated financial statements of Al Hilal Bank, at the end of 2019, Kazakhstan's share in the group's Islamic financial operations reached 8.2%.

Kazakhstan's Al Hilal has been operating on the market for 10 years. In this regard, it is appropriate to summarize some of the results of its work based on the analysis of financial reports for 2010–2019, available on the Bank's website:

- the Bank's assets grow by 20% annually (CAGR) amounting to 34 bln tenge (about $90 mln) by the end of 2019);
- the assets are mainly formed by accounts receivable under murabaha agreements and cash and equivalents, which, in turn, are placed on current accounts with commercial banks and the National Bank of Kazakhstan in the form of tawarruq[3];
- accounts receivable under murabaha agreements are mainly represented by the corporate sector, but in 2019 the retail part of it, issued in the form of Islamic mortgages, increased more than 5 times and amounted to almost 2 bln tenge (about $5 mln);
- since 2016, the Bank receives at least a quarter of its revenue from Islamic financial transactions in the interbank market in the form of tawarruq (Fig. 1.2);

---

[1] Al Hilal Bank was established by the Government of Abu Dhabi in the UAE in 2007.
[2] https://www.alhilalbank.ae/en/news/2019/april/al-hilal-bank-embarks-on-digital-transformation-1.aspx
[3] Tawarruq is an Islamic financial agreement for the purchase of deferred payment and sale of the same product to a 3rd party at the spot price. It is used by many Islamic banks for liquidity management.

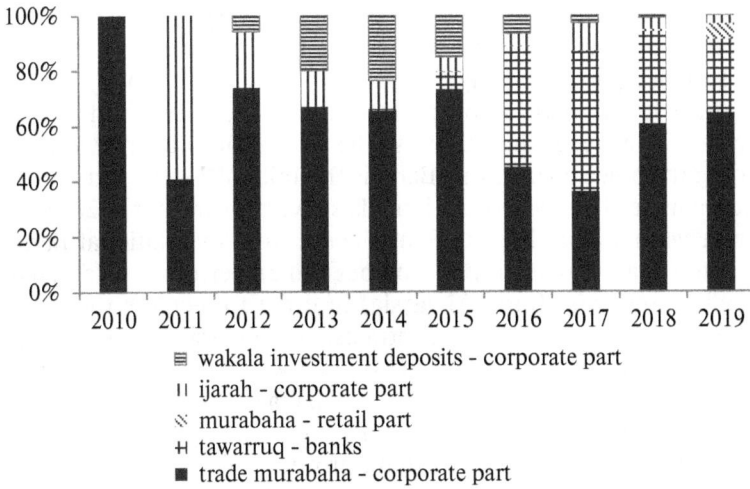

Fig. 1.2. Structure of the Bank's income
from Islamic Finance transactions

- wakala investment deposits - corporate part
- ijarah - corporate part
- murabaha - retail part
- tawarruq - banks
- trade murabaha - corporate part

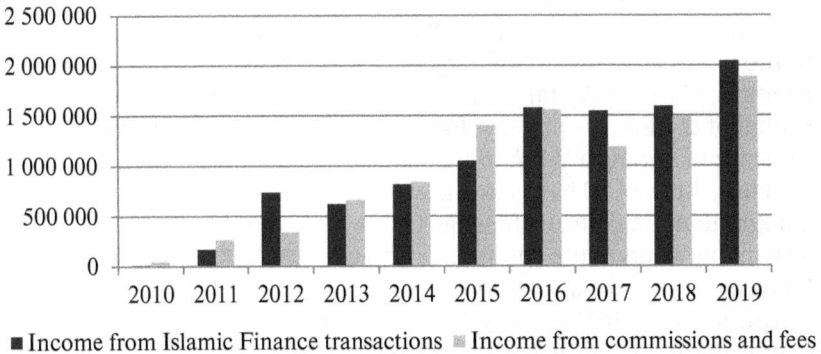

■ Income from Islamic Finance transactions ■ Income from commissions and fees

Fig.1.3. Bank's income from Islamic Finance transactions
and commissions and fees, th tenge
Source: compiled from annual audited reports Al HilalBank, PJSC[1]

- in recent years, the role of wakala investment deposits and Islamic leasing (ijarah) in the corporate sector has been reduced due to the increase in the share of Islamic interbank operations of tawarruq;
- the Bank's commission income is comparable to the income from Islamic Finance activities (Fig.1.3).

---

[1] https://alhilalbank.kz/en/page/reporting

In 2013, one of the oldest banks in Kazakhstan, *Zaman Bank* (founded in 1991), decides to fully convert to an Islamic Bank and signs a strategic partnership agreement with ICD (IDB group), which in exchange for a contribution of $10 mln to the authorized capital receives a 5% share of the business (the rest belongs to individuals). According to some sources, this Bank is the initiator of the 3rd law on Islamic Finance. The transformation takes several years, but in 2017 the Bank receives a special Islamic Bank license from the National Bank. In the same year, Zaman Bank becomes a member of the Malaysian commodity exchange (Bursa Malaysia) in order to increase the scope of operations under murabaha contracts. An analysis of the Bank's financial statements available on the official website[1] shows that 96% of all revenues are derived from trade murabaha contracts, with 98% of them coming from the corporate sector. Thus, the Bank's initial plans to become the first Islamic retail Bank proved difficult to implement. Nevertheless, Zaman Bank is a fairly successful enterprise: its revenue from Islamic financing increased 8 times over the year (from 112 to 872 mln tenge). This, in turn, allowed to increase assets by 11% (up to 15 bln tenge, which is more than $43.5 mln).

In the spring of 2020, *Masraf Al Rayan*, the ninth largest Islamic Bank in the world and the second largest in Qatar by assets, announced the creation of a fully digital Islamic Bank in Kazakhstan. The authorized capital of the Bank is planned to be $20 mln. The project is currently at the stage of signing a 'Memorandum of Understanfing.

Thus, 2 out of 30 banks in Kazakhstan are Islamic. Their total assets amount to more than 50 bln tenge (about $145.5 mln), which is 0.2 % of all banking assets in the country. On the one hand, this figure is certainly far from the initial expectations of the authorities. However, what seems insignificant at the 'industry level' turns out to be quite a successful enterprise at the 'firm level'. But the common drawback of Islamic banks in Kazakhstan is being mainly focused on the murabaha contracts and dealing mostly with businesses, leaving the individuals out. Low awareness of the Kazakhstan residents about Islamic Finance remains one of the main problems of the sector. Thus, according to a survey conducted in 2015 by Thomson Reuters (2015), 71% of respondents still have never heard of Islamic banking/Finance. If Islamic banks conduct extensive marketing and educational activities among the population, they have every chance to occupy a more significant niche in the market. However, the experience of Malaysia shows that a sharp growth of

---

[1] http://zamanbank.kz/en/o-banke/

Islamic banking in the consumer sector is facilitated by opening Islamic windows within conventional banks. However, the National Bank of Kazakhstan refused this approach, and preferred to issue separate licenses to Islamic banks.

THE ISSUE OF ISLAMIC BONDS (SUKUK)

Since 2010 the government of Kazakhstan intended to issue Islamic bonds (sukuk) in order to set a benchmark for the corporate sector. The authorities expected that the state-owned KazAgro, Kazpost, ProdCorporation, and after that private companies will enter this market. The first placement of sovereign securities by the Kazakh government took place in 2012, after the adoption of the 2nd package of laws allowing sovereign and quasi-sovereign institutions to issue Islamic securities[1]. Noteworthy, this was the first sovereign sukuk in the entire post-Soviet area. The issuer was a development institute — Development Bank of Kazakhstan. It issued a *5-year sukuk al-Murabaha* based on commodities with a profit margin of 5.5%. The volume of output amounted 240mln Malaysian ringgit (more than $75 mln) within the planned 1.5 bln-worth medium term program. As it can be seen, the bonds were denominated in Malaysian ringgit. The output was modest: e.g., in 2014 South Africa issued $500 mln sovereign sukuk, Luxembourg — $220 mln, and Hong Kong — $1 bln. Capital in Kazakhstan was not only attracted according to Islamic principles, but also placed in the same way: it is known that in 2016 Development Bank of Kazakhstan provided Islamic leasing financing (ijarah) to Istcomtrans for the purchase of tank cars in the amount of 1.1 bln tenge (more than $3 mln). Sukuk allocation took place in parallel in two countries: on the Kazakh stock exchange KASE and in Malaysia. More than a third (38%) of the issue was purchased by Kazakh investors (mainly the Pension Fund of Kazakhstan), and the rest (62%) was purchased by Malaysian investors. The issue was organized by Malaysian Islamic banks: the Royal Bank of Scotland Berhad, HSBC Amanah Malaysia Berhad, and Kazakhstan's Halyk Finance. Worthy of attention is that no securities of this sovereign sukuk were purchased by Al Hilal, the only Islamic Bank in Kazakhstan at that time. However, in the Bank's reports for 2012, we see that the Bank invested in a less profitable sukuk of two Emirati banks in the amount of $20 mln: First Gulf Bank and Abu Dhabi Investment Bank with an expected profit

---

[1] Referred to Law No. 475-IV of July 22, 2011 'On Amendments and Additions to Certain Legislative Acts of the Republic of Kazakhstan on the Organization of Islamic Finance'.

rate of 4.046 and 3.78% which expired in 2017 and 2016, respectively. Apparently, this was the investment decision of the Al Hilal head office in the UAE.

"<...>This is a major achievement for both the Bank and Kazakhstan <...> to promote our credit history in Malaysia and strengthen the authority of the Republic of Kazakhstan in the Islamic investment community. We are convinced that this transaction will open the way for other issuers in the region to diversify their funding in the Islamic markets", the Bank's management commented on this deal[1]. D. Hoggarth (2016) in his work notes: "For Malaysia, the development of another market player appears to have created a mutually beneficial relationship rather than a potentially hostile competitor". It is possible that at that time the focus was on building new investment relationships, but as we will see later, these plans were never to come true.

In 2015, the country's officials announced the imminent release of $3 bln sukuk, where the base asset was to be the Astana–Burabay toll road[2]. In 2018, some intentions were expressed on a new issue of sovereign sukuk for $300 mln[3]. However, since then, no new placements of sovereign sukuk have taken place, even within the above-mentioned $1.5 bln program.

In the spring of 2020, the world's fifth-largest international Islamic Bank (*Qatar International Islamic Bank*) placed a $500 mln sukuk on the London (LSE) and Astana (AIX)[4] stock exchanges. The buyers of sukuk are unknown, but for the Astana exchange, this was the debut placement of sukuk. However, the issue of Islamic bonds (sukuk) has not become a widespread practice for Kazakh businesses to attract financing, and the purchase of the 2012 sovereign issue by Malaysian investors looks more like a gesture of goodwill. On the technical side, this situation can be explained by some complexity of structuring sukuk deals (the search for the underlying asset and its ability to bring sufficient profit to investors), which encourages issuers to use interest-based methods of financing. Another preventing factor is lack of broad and diverse economic ties with Malaysia and Saudi Arabia which account for 37.9 and 33.1% of all international sukuk issues, respectively (IFSB, 2018).

---

[1] https://sk.kz/ifswf/news/company/7806/
[2] https://cbonds.ru/news/796819/
[3] https://vlast.kz/novosti/23597-v-2018-godu-kazakhstan-planiruet-vypustit-cennye-bumagi-sukuk-do-300-mln-dollarov.html
[4] Shareholders of the Astana stock exchange (AIX), among others, include the Shanghai stock exchange (SSE), US companies Nasdaq and Goldman Sachs.

ISLAMIC LEASING (IJARAH) COMPANIES

Of all the types of Islamic Finance, Islamic leasing is perhaps the least different from conventional financial leasing. However, Islamic leasing companies carry greater risks than conventional leasing companies because:

- lease payments start from the date of putting the equipment in operation (not from the date of contract conclusion);
- in case of equipment failure caused by the manufacturer, lease payments to the lessor are suspended;
- in case of late lease payments fines are directed to charity instead of charging against the income of the Islamic leasing company.

Today, there are more than 20 leasing companies on the Kazakhstan market, 2 of which are Islamic these are the already mentioned KIC leasing and Al Saqr Finance. The first company was founded in 2013, its shareholders are 6 organizations: the IDB owns a 36% through ICD; subsidiaries of the two above-mentioned Islamic banks Zaman Leasing (18%) and Al Hilal Leasing (14%); Turkish Aktif Bank (14%); Korean private equity fund Kolon Investment (11%) and the distributor of American agricultural machinery Eurasia Group AG (7%). As mentioned above, in 2013 The IDB allocated $10 mln to *KIC leasing*. In 2019, according to the murabaha standard, the company received more than $67 mln from its shareholder. It is known that in 2017, KIC leasing completed 36 deals, and Al Saqr Finance did 16, while the volume of the leasing portfolio for both companies increased significantly over the same year: by 85% to 5.7 bln tenge for KIC leasing and by 71% to 2.65 bln tenge for Al Saqr Finance[1]. Only one deal of KIC leasing, the financing of the positron emission tomography center at Kazakh Research Institute of Oncology and Radiology, was covered in the media[2]. KIC leasing does not publish its financial statements, but, according to the company's top manager, over 5 years of operation, they have developed a base of more than 170 clients and provided financing for more than $40 mln in various sectors of the economy, from medicine to construction[3].

Special attention should be paid to *Al Saqr Finance*. Operating on the market since 2000 as BTA Leasing (the sole shareholder of the company

---

[1] https://expertonline.kz/a15634/
[2] https://forbes.kz/process/medicine/v_almatyi_privezli_noveyshuyu_tehniku_dlya_ranney_diagnostiki_onkologii/
[3] https://forbes.kz/finances/finance/islamskiy_lizing_kak_alternativa_bankovskomu_kreditovaniyu/

was BTA Bank, now the company is owned by individuals), then renamed SK Leasing, in 2016 the company decides to transform into an Islamic financial company. Since 2017, it begins to provide Islamic leasing services: during the year, Al Saqr Finance financed 16 projects for 2.65 bln tenge (more than $6 mln), including the purchase of real estate by the state company TransTeleCom (office premises with an area of 3,000 sq m). Analyzing the company's reporting data, we see that during the year the business of Islamic leasing operations increased by 40%, and profitability increased to 16%[1]. In 2019, jointly with Kazakhstan's ForteBank, the company issued the first Islamic payment cards (applications for cards are submitted via the website goislamic.kz). The company's 2017 annual audited report stated that its goal was to attract a strategic Islamic investor and further convert Al Saqr into an Islamic Bank by 2020–2021. It should be recognized that the company is steadily moving towards this goal — at the end of 2019, Al Saqr Finance signed a Memorandum of Cooperation with ICD (IDB group).

ISLAMIC INSURANCE (TAKAFUL) COMPANIES

Islamic insurance (takaful) is the least developed segment of the global Islamic financial market. But, nevertheless, from 2012 to 2016, this market grew by 8.8% per year, and due to the low penetration of insurance services, as well as the growing welfare of the Muslim population in the world, it is viewed as promising (IFSB, 2018). The main markets for takaful are Saudi Arabia (38%) and Iran (34%).

The only Islamic insurance company on the territory of the CIS countries, *Mutual Halal Insurance Society Takaful*, was launched in Kazakhstan, in 2010, the year of opening of the first Islamic Bank Al Hilal. However, from the first days of its operation the company faced legal difficulties: it was the moment of introducing changes in the legislation on insurance activities prohibiting mutual insurance companies to transfer their risks to reinsurance companies. That is why Mutual Halal Insurance Society Takaful failed to fully realize its potential providing just a limited set of takaful services to the individuals. Over the years of operation on the market, from 2010 to 2016, the company provided medical insurance, car insurance, and hajj travel insurance. 'Takaful' had a client base of more than 3,000 people. It is also known that the company had plans to attract a strategic Islamic investor, but due to new changes in legislation that prohibited mutual insurance companies from

---

[1] https://alsaqr.kz/about/reports

providing takaful services, it had to close down after 7 years of operation. Active fundraising activities of this company contributed to attracting many foreign takaful companies to the Kazakh market. But their entry into the local market required special legislation. In 2015, some changes were made with the 3rd package of laws on Islamic Finance, but still, no takaful companies are represented on the Kazakh market today.

PRIVATE EQUITY FUNDS

In conventional financial systems, Islamic investors prefer to work through private equity funds, which in their economic essence are similar to Islamic financial instruments (Nagimova, 2018a). Kazakhstan has repeatedly announced the creation of joint private equity funds with sovereign funds of the Persian Gulf countries. However, only one project has come to life: a joint fund *Al Falah Capital*, where the UAE investor was represented by International Petroleum Investment Company, which is owned by the government of Abu Dhabi. Despite the fact that the declared amount of the Fund was $500 mln, over 5 years of operation, it invested only in 3 projects — the construction of two poultry farms and the reconstruction of a thermal power plant[1]. Of course, some of the deals may have not been publicly disclosed, but the number of projects financed by the Fund is still small, which casts doubt on the declared size and scale of the Fund's work.

It is also known that in 2011, the *Islamic Infrastructure Fund* invested in the Kazakhstan market (the Fund's investors are the IDB, the Asian Development Bank, and Kazakhstan's Samruk-Kazyna). The Fund is managed by Singapore-based CapAsia which invested $50mln for a 13% stake in the Central Asian Electric Power Corporation operating in Kazakhstan. The funds received were used to upgrade the company's equipment. In early 2019, the Fund and the European Bank for Reconstruction and Development sold their stakes and exited this asset[2].

Thus, the sponsor of the 1st out of 27 private equity funds operating in Kazakhstan is an Arab investor. This Fund is actually quasi-sovereign and lacks a clear strategy for exits with the maximum return for its sponsors (LP, limited partner). This feature reflects the financial system of Kazakhstan as a whole which is characterized by a high concentration of the state capital.

---

[1] http://www.afcp.kz/en/portfolio.php
[2] https://inbusiness.kz/ru/news/ebrr-otkazalsya-svyazyvat-vyhod-iz-kapitala-caek-so-snizheniem-energotarifa

ASTANA INTERNATIONAL FINANCIAL CENTER (AIFC)

Despite the personal support of N. Nazarbayev, at the end of 2015, the National Bank of Kazakhstan refuses to further promote the Islamic Finance industry, and the specialized department ceases its activities. The Astana International Financial Center (AIFC), officially opened in 2018 in the form of a special economic zone, takes over the main agenda for the promotion of Islamic Finance. a benchmark for the AIFC was the Dubai International Financial Centre in the UAE ranking 8th in The Global Financial Centers Index (Z/Yen, 2019). Islamic Finance becomes one of the 6 strategic directions of the AIFC development[1]. For this purpose, the AIFC undertakes creating international councils, holding Islamic Finance Week, and arranging a number of educational programs. Finally, Kazakhstan receives a sovereign rating from the Islamic International Rating Agency. These efforts were noticed by the global Islamic financial community: in 2018, the AIFC ranks 24th (31st a year earlier) in the Global Islamic Finance Report Ranking and receives 3 awards from the Global Islamic Finance Awards. Thus, we see that the AIFC authorities are trying to create full-fledged institutional conditions for the development of the Islamic Finance industry.

It is noteworthy that one of the largest development projects in Nur-Sultan, *Abu Dhabi Plaza*, is being built by Arab investors. According to the project's investors themselves, $1.09 bln[2] was invested in the construction of the tallest building in Central Asia with a height of 75 floors. Despite the rather lengthy work that has already taken about 10 years (instead of the 4 planned), the Abu Dhabi Plaza complex is scheduled to open in 2020.

Thus, based on the analysis of more than 250 deals involving Islamic capital in Kazakhstan, the following trends can be identified:

- *first,* the main channel for attracting Islamic investment to the country is the IDB and the Abu Dhabi government (the latter is the ultimate owner of Al Hilal Bank and the Abu Dhabi Plaza, as well as a co-investor of the Al Falah Private Equity Fund);
- *second,* Islamic banks and Islamic leasing companies, although not yet taking up a significant market share, are nevertheless becoming an important market segment;
- *third,* despite the existing precedents, the potential for issuing Islamic bonds and Islamic insurance has not yet been fully realized;

---

[1] https://aifc.kz/uploads/AIFC_Annual_%20report_short_eng.pdf
[2] https://gulfbusiness.com/abu-dhabis-aldar-awards-1-1bn-contract-to-arabtec/

- *fourth,* although private equity funds with Arab investors are represented, they lack activity;
- *fifth,* having chosen Islamic Finance as one of the six areas of development, the AIFC has a chance to become a driver of this industry in the country.

In general, we confirm the arguments of A. Wolters (2013) and D. Hoggarth (2016) that Islamic Finance in Kazakhstan is an initiative that develops "from top to bottom", and the state is the key structure that makes decisions on the development of this sector of the financial market. Indeed, strategically speaking, "Islamic Finance will help to deliver this by raising Kazakhstan's international profile and projecting positive images, despite the country's record of market nepotism and corruption", as well as provide "an alternative source of foreign direct investment and new opportunities for political alliances that are unconnected to Russian and Chinese interests" (Hoggarth, 2016).

To sum it up, the total volume of investments with the participation of Islamic capital in Kazakhstan is estimated at more than $3.6 bln. Despite a small share of the occupied market, Islamic Finance has certainly greatly enriched the country's financial ecosystem. However, the market is still far from deep and saturated, which, at a minimum, requires a broader coverage of the population with Islamic financial services. This is the first factor for the development of the industry. Some optimism about the future of Islamic Finance in Kazakhstan is inspired by research conducted by Thomson Reuters (2015) among 1,500 respondents: the greatest interest in Islamic Finance is shown by the younger generation of Kazakhs[1]. In addition, the results of this research show that the growth driver of the industry will be Muslims, which is more than 70% of the population of Kazakhstan (more than 13 mln people). To meet the needs of such a market, the primary need is professional personnel, both local and foreign, who are able to use the full range of Islamic financial instruments. This is the next limiting factor in the market development, and the AIFC's educational programs are designed to solve the problem. a critical mass of professionals in the field of Islamic Finance should increase competition, while the entrepreneurial spirit and creative approach to business will both help to learn from the experience of other countries, and bring something new and different to the industry, as it can be seen from Malaysia's example.

---

[1] 8% of respondents over the age of 54, 42% — aged 25 to 54, and 49%— aged 18 to 34 answered the question 'Have you used the services or products of an Islamic financial institution?' positively.

CHAPTER 2.
UZBEKISTAN

... we have not been able to convince people that Islam is light...

Sh. Mirziyoyev

2nd President of Uzbekistan

To date, Uzbekistan with the population of more than 30 mln people is the most densely populated and the second largest state in Central Asia after Kazakhstan in terms of area and size of economy. Moreover, Uzbekistan is one of the fastest growing and most promising economies in the post-Soviet region. Thus, according to April, 2020 forecasts of the International Monetary Fund[1], the GDP of the Republic of Uzbekistan will grow by 1.8% in 2020. This is one of the highest rates in the CIS countries[2]. High expectations for the growth rate of the economy of this country are due, first of all, to the new leader. The acting president of Uzbekistan, Sh. Mirziyoyev, in contrast to his predecessor, I. Karimov, demonstrates a bolder approach to economic reforms[3]. This is clearly seen in the development of the Islamic Finance industry. Thus, according to A. Wolters (2013), a professor of OSCE, in the time of I. Karimov, Uzbekistan "seems to be a very sensitive environment for any project that bears the word Islamic in its title", but now the situation has begun to change. The approach of the new president is characterized by his words during a visit to the mausoleum of Sultan Saodat near Termez: "With so much knowledge and wealth, we have not been able to convince people that Islam is light. This is our tragedy"[4]. In 2018, for the first time in the country's history, a draft presidential decree on the Creation of an Islamic Financial Infrastructure and an Islamic Bank in Uzbekistan was submitted for public discussion. However, despite the history of Islamic Finance in Uzbekistan being less rich and diverse than, for example, in neighboring Kazakhstan or Kyrgyzstan, a strict scientific approach allowed us to compile and analyze an empirical base consisting of about 400 deals with Islamic capital, and to identify the following:

---

[1] https://www.imf.org/external/datamapper/NGDP_RPCH@WEO/OEMDC/ADVEC/WEOWORLD

[2] While the economies of other countries will shrink: for example, Kazakhstan — by 2.5%, Azerbaijan — by 2.2%, Kyrgyzstan — by 4%, Russia — by 5.5%.

[3] https://eiu.bvdep.com

[4] https://www.gazeta.uz/ru/2019/04/10/islam/

ISLAMIC DEVELOPMENT BANK GROUP

Having gained state sovereignty, in the 1990s Uzbekistan, along with the other CIS countries with a predominantly Muslim population[1], joined the Organization of the Islamic Conference (was renamed to the Organization of Islamic Cooperation in 2011). However, the Republic became a member of the Islamic Development Bank (IDB) later than all other post-Soviet countries — only in 2003. (Appendix B). After joining the IDB, the first lines of financing were allocated to two institutions of the financial sector of the country: Ipak Yuli Bank and Uzbek Leasing International (Aliyev, 2012).

As mentioned above, the policy of the former Uzbek government regarding everything related to Islam was always suspicious, and Islamic Finance was no exception[2]. Even before Uzbekistan's official membership, the IDB sent small grants there, for example, to restore madrassas and dormitories at Mir-Arab and Dar El-Hadith madrassas in the ancient city of Bukhara, as well as to purchase medical equipment for surgical departments. According to our calculations, the IDB allocated a total of just over $1.6 mln to Uzbekistan for the implementation of these projects until 2003. However, after the country became a full member of the IDB, the cooperation turned into financing of periodic 3-year development programs of the country.

Our analysis showed that the country has attracted almost $2 bln of investment from the IDB for the implementation of more than 100 projects (besides the investments from its subsidiaries). The average size of the IDB deals in Uzbekistan, therefore, was more than $19 mln (Appendix B). At the same time, the country's share in the bank's subscribed capital is 0.03% ($13.4 mln). It should be mentioned that among all the CIS countries, it was Uzbekistan that attracted the most capital from this development bank. After all, despite the fact that the economy of Uzbekistan is 3 times smaller than that of neighboring Kazakhstan, almost half of the population of the Central Asia lives in this country.

We found out that more than 75% of the finance attracted to Uzbekistan from the IDB (see Table 2.1) was allocated across four sectors — industry, housing construction, finance and water supply. In addition, the bank invested in road construction, healthcare, energy, education, and public administration.

---

[1] According to the Pew Research Center (2015), 97.1% of the population of Uzbekistan is Muslim. Moreover, Uzbekistan has been one of the centers of Islamic thought for many centuries. In the Republic, 90% of about 4,000 historical monuments are monuments of Islamic culture.

[2] A. Wolters (2013) connects this, first of all, with the events in Andijan in the Ferghana valley in May 2005.

Table 2.1. The IDB deals in Uzbekistan

Sector	Number of IDB deals, pcs.	Total investment by the IDB, $ mln	Share in total investment, %
Industry	40	413	20.7
Housing construction	4	400	20.1
Finance	23	384	19.3
Water supply and irrigation	5	325	16.3
Road construction	2	180	9
Healthcare	9	109	5.5
Energy	3	99	5
Education and science	12	79	4
Public administration	5	1	0.05
Total	103	1,990	99.95

Source: calculation based on Appendix C.

For the IDB the largest investment projects in Uzbekistan were the Development of Housing Construction in Rural Areas Project (the total investment of the IDB was more than $400 mln), the purchase of two aircrafts for Uzbek airlines (more than $168 mln) and the reconstruction of the M39 highway (more than $167 mln), which together account for more than a third of all the investments of the IDB allocated in this country.

Each of more than 100 projects financed by the IDB in Uzbekistan (Appendix C) is very important, but here we will focus on only one of them — financing *the Housing Construction in Rural Areas Program*, which is the largest and unique. This program was initiated by the government of Uzbekistan in 2009 and was caused by a shortage of living space per capita in rural areas. The natural and migration[1] growth of the rural population of the country made this problem even more acute. The expected result of the project is the construction of 75,000 standard modern individual residential buildings by 2021. In total, the program costs $2.7 bln. Since 2012, the program was funded by the Asian Development Bank for a total of $500 mln. The co-investor of the program was the IDB, which invested more than $400mln in three tranches in the project. That was done in the form of istisna[2]. We know

---

[1] The Asian Development Bank (2016a) estimates that 330,000 migrants, mostly from Russia, returned to Uzbekistan in 2014—2015.

[2] Istisna is a long-term Islamic financial agreement for the construction or manufacture of some asset with an obligation to deliver them to the buyer upon completion. The

from the media that in 2017 the IDB granted Uzbekistan the second tranche of $300 mln for a 15-year period, including a 2-year grace period. In addition, the project was invested by the IDB partners in the Arab Coordination Group[1] — The Saudi Fund for Development ($110 mln in three tranches) and The Kuwait Fund for Arab Economic Development ($30 mln). Besides housing construction, the investors' funds were allocated to renovation of the roads, gas, electricity and water supply networks, sports grounds, schools, medical institutions, shops and bus stops. The money went to the state construction company Qishlok Qurilish Invest and to mortgage financing of the population through six Uzbek banks. Preferential mortgages for the purchase of apartments in these houses were provided to young families, residents of dilapidated houses and other categories of needy citizens for up to 15 years. Mortgage financing was issued with a 3-year grace period with an margin of 7% per annum for the first 5 years and a refinancing rate of the Central Bank of Uzbekistan for the subsequent period. This large-scale program enhanced the emergence of rural residential clusters as well as the growth of the financial sector (due to increased mortgage financing), the construction industry and the creation of new jobs.

So, we have conducted a detailed analysis of each of the IDB deals in Uzbekistan based on all publicly available information, including participants, investors, the volume and terms of their financing, and identified a number of patterns:

- *first,* the IDB provides Uzbekistan with preferential long-term financing for up to 16 years, of which a maximum of 4 years are usually grace period;
- *second,* the IDB often participates in deals in a consortium with other international development banks: the World Bank, the Asian Development Bank, the European Bank for Reconstruction and Development, and others;
- *third,* the IDB engages other members of the Arab Coordination Group (Saudi Fund for Development, the OPEC Fund for International Development, the Kuwait Fund for Arab Economic Development[2]) in its deals. On one hand, that allows to diversify

---

advantage of istisna is that payments by the client can be made in installments, after delivery or completion of the project.

[1] The Arab Coordination Group is an informal association of bilateral and multilateral development institutions in the Gulf countries.

[2] From 1997 to 2018 the Kuwait Fund for Arab Economic Development provided Uzbekistan with $183.1 mln in concessional financing for the implementation of 9 social projects and $2.4 mln in grants for the preparation of feasibility studies for 5 projects.

risks between project investors, on the other hand — to establish bilateral investment cooperation between countries;

- *fourth,* the condition for providing capital from the IDB is co-financing by the local government in a ratio of at least 1:4 (local government funds: the IDB investments), including tax benefits and other mandatory payments to the country's budget;
- *fifth,* a greater part of the IDB's investment is directed at financing physical infrastructure for housing, water supply, road construction, medicine, energy sector, and education;
- *sixth,* in Uzbekistan, unlike the other CIS countries, the IDB has financed a large number of deals in the industrial sector, which is probably due to the fact that the share of small and medium-sized businesses in the country's GDP increased within 16 years: from 31% in 2000 to 57% in 2016 (EBRD, 2018);
- *seventh,* the IDB has only allocated funding to Uzbekistan for the establishment of international research centers to study, for example, the religious and spiritual heritage of Imam al-Bukhari's Islamic culture in Samarkand ($280,000 in 2018) and the environmental impacts of the drying up of the Aral sea ($278,000 in 2019).

ISLAMIC BANKS

In mid-2018, a presidential decree announced creating an infrastructure for Islamic banking and finance in Uzbekistan[1]. For this purpose a special commission was organized. Their task was to prepare a draft decision of the President on the establishment of an Islamic Bank that provides a wide range of financial services, including export-import and housing financing, leasing, insurance and services in the securities market. In May 2019 The Cabinet of Ministers of the Republic of Uzbekistan issued a resolution 'On Measures for Further Development of Cooperation with the Group of the Islamic Development Bank and the Funds of the Arab Coordination Group'. It was also supposed to attract a grant from the IDB to create a legal framework for the full operation of the Islamic financial infrastructure in the country.

After the publication of these documents in 2019 several Uzbek banks announced their intention to develop Islamic banking in the form of an Islamic window. Those were state-owned Uzpromstroybank, Qishlok Qurilish Bank, Trustbank, and private Kapitalbank and Ipak Yuli Bank.

Moreover, according to the press service of Trustbank, they held talks with the providers of IT-service for the operation of the Islamic window, and Ipak Yuli Bank officially signed a Memorandum at the 44th meeting of the IDB, which was held in Morocco.

The creation of the Islamic window was not a spontaneous decision of the management of Uzbek banks. That was preceded by extensive experience in attracting financing from the IDB subsidiaries. First of all, from the Islamic Corporation for Private Sector Development (ICD) and the International Islamic Trade and Finance Corporation (ITFC). Both of the organizations provide Islamic financing for the development of small and medium-sized businesses; the first provides medium-term capital (up to 5 years) for the purchase of fixed assets (technology and equipment), and the second — short-term capital (up to 1 year) for the purchase of goods and raw materials. At the same time, it is ICD that has the broadest experience of investment cooperation with Uzbek banks. According to our calculations, since 2006, ICD has provided financing to 15 of the 30 banks operating in Uzbekistan, while ITFC has provided only 5 banks. We estimate the amount of capital allocated by ITFC at $38 mln. The amount of capital provided to Uzbek banks by ICD is quite difficult to estimate accurately, since it is often 'mixed' with the capital of the 'parent' structure — the IDB, but we suppose it to be $164.5 mln at least.

As mentioned above, in 2006 *Ipak Yuli Bank* (from the Uzbek — 'Silk Road') was the first among Uzbek banks, after the country's accession to the IDB, to receive Islamic capital in the amount of $2 mln from ICD. Since then, the bank has raised more than $20 mln from ICD, and at the 'Days of the IDB Group' held in September 2018 in Tashkent it received an award as the 'Best ICD Partner'. However, the most impressive results with the help of financing from ICD were achieved by two other banks: *Asaka Bank*, that started cooperation in 2009, attracted more than $31 mln, which was used to implement 22 projects and create more than 1,000 new jobs[1]. *Qishlok Qurilish Bank* (from the Uzbek — 'Rural Construction'), having started cooperation in 2010, attracted $21 mln and financed the largest number of projects, for which it received the same award at the 'Days of the IDB Group' in Tashkent.

As for the amount of funding from ICD, at the very beginning of cooperation, in 2006, the Corporation allocated $2 mln for each bank, then, by 2017, for a number of banks it increased to $12 mln. This

---

[1] https://www.asakabank.uz/ru/press-centr/meropriyatiya/provedena_press_konferenciya_o_provedennyh_rabotah_bankom_asaka_po

indicates the enhanced credibility for the market and its participants on the part of the Islamic investor.

Turning to the issue of Islamic Finance from ITFC, it should be noted that it is short-term trade financing, usually directed to foreign trade operations of businesses. We estimate its volume at $38 mln, of which the largest funding line of $15 mln was allocated to *Uzpromstroybank* in early 2019.

The allocation of the capital from both of the IDB subsidiaries — ICD and ITFC — among small and medium-sized businesses in Uzbekistan was made in the form of murabaha. Uzbek banks have not yet used risky financial instruments such as *mudaraba* or *musharaka*[1].

Kh. Khasanov, the representative of the IDB in the Republic of Uzbekistan, noted that "Islamic banking can attract up to $10 bln to Uzbekistan annually, if the necessary legislation becomes available"[2]. In his opinion, the introduction of Islamic banking in Uzbekistan will help attract resources from the population in addition to foreign investment. This point of view can be supported by the International Monetary Fund estimates that only 10% of the population's private savings are placed in Uzbek banks, which is significantly less than in more developed economies in transition. However, in order to expand funding for the needs of a growing economy, banks will need to build individuals' confidence in the sector (IMF, 2019b).

In general, the problem with the country's banking system is that large state-owned banks account for 85% of total assets. These banks are actually agents of government programs and development plans, and disproportionately lend to the public sector, which accounts for more than 50% of their loan portfolios. The other banks, including 5 banks with foreign participation, operate in more market conditions (EBRD, 2018). The banking sector in Uzbekistan is relatively large, but the high concentration of the sector around state-owned banks and government lending restricts access to the capital outside of government programs. Thus, despite the double-digit growth rate of lending over the past 5 years, the availability of finance is the main problem for small and medium-sized businesses. The IMF survey (2019b) showed that in 2017 only

---

[1] Equity types of Islamic financing, the first of which is a deal where one party provides capital, and the other manages the project, while the profits are distributed in a predetermined ratio, and the investor is responsible for losses; the second type of financing is a joint venture in which each party provides capital for its implementation, while the profits are distributed among the participants in proportion to their contribution, and the losses — according to the agreement of the parties.

[2] https://uz.sputniknews.ru/economy/20190416/11251847/V-IBR-obsnili-pochemu-Uzbekistanu-nuzhno-razvivat-islamskiy-banking.html

about 25% of small and medium-sized businesses developed through bank loans, and more than 80% of them financed their investments from their own resources. This is significantly higher than in other Central Asian countries.

ISLAMIC LEASING (IJARAH) COMPANIES

In 2010 *the Islamic leasing company Taiba Leasing* was established. The company's sole shareholder is the above-mentioned ICD, which is part of the IDB Group. The shareholder's contribution to the capital of Taiba Leasing was $5 mln. The data on ICD operations show that in 2013 and 2016 this Corporation opened financing lines for its subsidiary leasing company in the form of istisna and murabaha for a aggregate of $10 mln[1]. Taiba Leasing clients are small and medium-sized businesses. In 2017 the size of its leasing portfolio exceeded 61 bln sum (about $12 mln), and the number of contracts — 120. In terms of the volume of its portfolio and the number of deals in 2016 Taiba Leasing was one of the four largest leasing companies in Uzbekistan, but in the following years lost its leadership.

Besides Taiba Leasing Islamic financing was also allocated to *Uzbek Leasing International*, a conventional leasing company, which was founded in 1996 by the Malaysian Maybank[2], The National Bank for Foreign Economic Affairs of the Republic of Uzbekistan, the European Bank for Reconstruction and Development, and the International Finance Corporation. Uzbek Leasing International is the largest leasing company in the country. The company is currently owned by Maybank (35%), The National Bank for Foreign Economic Affairs of the Republic of Uzbekistan (35%) and UzOmanCapital (30%). The European Bank for Reconstruction and Development and the International Finance Corporation sold their shares to the latter in 2013. The company finances leasing deals both from its own funds and the funds of shareholders, as well as from the financing lines of international development institutions: the European Bank for Reconstruction and Development, the Asian Development Bank, and others. Since 2006 Uzbek Leasing International attracted three lines of Islamic financing

---

[1] https://icd-ps.org/en/projects-summary
[2] One of the largest banks in Malaysia and South-East Asia, both in terms of assets and capitalization. 2,400 offices of the bank are located in 15 countries. The Bank's Islamic division, Maybank Islamic Berhad, is the world's 5th largest bank by assets and controls a third of Malaysia's Islamic banking market. In recent years the business of Maybank Islamic has boomed in Indonesia. In addition, Maybank Islamic does business in Singapore, UAE and Hong Kong.

from the IDB for a total of $11 mln and one line from ICD for $5 mln and directed them to small and medium-sized business projects in the form of murabaha. In the spring of 2020 the company received the 'Best Murabaha Product' Award. According to the company's reports, Islamic Finance was directed to the implementation of 36 projects in such areas as medicine, food production, agriculture, production of building materials, construction, etc.[1]

Generally, the leasing financing market in Uzbekistan is still small, poorly developed, highly fragmented, and a third of it is provided by commercial banks. One of the main factors in the development of the leasing market is access to funding, including lines of financing from foreign banks and development institutions. However, in our opinion, it is more promising to expand the sources of financing for leasing companies in the securities market, for example, by issuing Islamic bonds (sukuk).

THE ISSUE OF ISLAMIC BONDS (SUKUK)

At the end of 2019 the Capital Markets Development Agency of the Republic of Uzbekistan presents the Capital Market Development Strategy for 2020–2025, developed by BTA and ISC consulting companies with the support of the European Bank for Reconstruction and Development and the Asian Development Bank, which have experience in promoting reforms in more than 50 countries. Then director of this Agency A. Nazarov announces the start of issuing Islamic bonds (sukuk) in mid-2020. According to the Roadmap for this Strategy, in 2020, with the technical assistance of the IDB, a legal act on Islamic bonds (sukuk) will be adopted. BTA and ISC consultants concluded that the issue of sukuk will help to attract additional funds to the economy from the 'shadow market'.

The Uzbek authorities are planning to develop the sukuk market together with the stock market. It is planned to adopt a single law 'On the Capital Market', which will combine more than 100 laws that currently regulate this market. In addition to sukuk, it is planned to introduce other financial instruments (exchange-traded investment funds, currency and commodity derivatives, corporate, municipal and mortgage bonds) on the stock market of Uzbekistan and ensure their secondary trading. The volume of securities freely traded on the Toshkent stock exchange is expected to increase from 0.4% to 10% of

---

[1] http://uzbekleasing.uz/en/about/news/2056/

GDP within 5 years. The Strategy provides guidelines: in Singapore, this figure is 188%, in Malaysia — 112%, in Russia — 34%. One of the goals is also to enter the rating of the Morgan Stanley Capital International (MSCI) World Index by 2025.

Full implementation of the Capital Market Development Strategy will eliminate unnecessary restrictions and simplify the work of investors in the stock market, which should ultimately reduce the dependence of the local economy on the banking sector. According to the calculations, a new class of retail investors will be created as a result of attracting 2.5 mln Uzbek citizens, whose investments will amount to 6% of their savings, which will eventually lead to an increase in their wealth.

A developed capital market is a crucially important component of the country's financial system. Thus, in 2017 25% of the shares of the Toshkent stock exchange were sold to a strategic investor — the Korean stock exchange (KRX). In 2020 "the possibility of handing over the controlling stake <...> to implement new technologies" was considered[1].

PRIVATE EQUITY FUNDS

As we have already seen in the previous Chapter, in conventional financial systems an alternative to Islamic financial structures can be private equity funds, which are based on the main principle of Islamic Finance — the principle of profit and loss sharing (Nagimova, 2018). In Uzbekistan several attempts have been made to create joint private equity funds between the local and Gulf countries governments. Thus, in 2008 they announce the creation of Uzemiratholding with the headquarters in Tashkent and assets under management in the amount of $1.25 bln, where Dubai Holding from the UAE intended to invest $1 bln, and the Fund for Reconstruction and Development of the Republic of Uzbekistan — $250 mln. However, we do not know anything about the deals of this joint fund. This suggests that the Fund, most likely, has not become fully operational. After 10 years the attempts were repeated: thus, in 2018 The National Bank for Foreign Economic Affairs of the Republic of Uzbekistan and the Abu Dhabi Fund for Development from the United Arab Emirates agreed to create a joint fund of $100 mln. The capital was planned to be used for the construction of a hotel and a shopping and entertainment center in Samarkand, which would increase the tourist potential of this ancient city. Besides, the joint fund was supposed to finance projects in such

---

[1] https://tashkenttimes.uz/finances/4907-controlling-stake-in-republican-stock-exchange-could-be-handed-over-to-korean-stock-exchange

areas as electricity and water supply, healthcare, agriculture, transport and others. In 2019 the Abu Dhabi Fund for Development and the Fund for Reconstruction and Development of the Republic of Uzbekistan announce the creation of an Uzbek-Emirati investment company with an authorized capital of $5 mln. This company is supposed to manage a fund with a declared capital of $300 mln. The share of the Uzbek side in the fund is 25%, and that of the Arab side — 75% (with the possibility of attracting additional participants: investment and financial companies from the UAE). According to the media, this fund will allocate funding to improve the infrastructure of Samarkand: roads and drinking water supply systems, and, in cooperation with The National Bank for Foreign Economic Affairs of the Republic of Uzbekistan, will build hotels and a shopping center in the city. This fund is also likely to remain in the status of a Declaration of Intent.

Unlike previous funds that were actually only 'on paper', UzOmanCapital is a 'live' fund that has been actively investing in Uzbekistan for 10 years. This fund was created in 2010 with initial capital of $100 mln. At the end of the life cycle of the fund, after 7 years (in 2017), it was recapitalized by another $100 mln. The fund's shareholders are State General Reserve Fund, the sovereign wealth fund of Oman (75%), and the Fund for Reconstruction and Development of Uzbekistan (25%). To date, UzOmanCapital has 9 companies in its portfolio, including the above-mentioned Uzbek Leasing International (that was the fund's first deal made in 2012). The fund provides direct long-term investments in the amount of $3–10 mln to private Uzbek companies. UzOmanCapital's portfolio companies are Polifleks and Polispertr (printing companies), Prime Ceramics, VMC (a galvanized product manufacturer), ULS (a container terminal), Dorkomplektsnab Services (a crushed stone manufacturer), a door and furniture manufacturer, and Temiryol Sugurta (an insurance company). In addition, UzOmanCapital is the founder and manager of the largest shopping and office centers in Uzbekistan: UzOmanTower, Samarqand Darvoza and Compass. According to the company, 3,720 new jobs were created through the fund's investments1. In 2019 UzOmanCapital also began to provide consulting services to potential investors in the Uzbek economy and launched an exchange traded fund.

So, we estimate the total volume of Islamic investments in the economy of Uzbekistan, involved in the implementation of more than 350 deals, at more than $2.5 bln. Islamic capital in Uzbekistan is formed by 92% of the investments of the Islamic Development Bank (including

---

[1] https://uoic.uz/ru/

its subsidiaries) and 8% of the sovereign wealth fund of Oman (through the UzOmanCapital private equity fund). It should be emphasized that over the past 15 years Islamic Finance in Uzbekistan has been slowly but consistently forming a new segment of the economy, which is impossible to ignore. As A. Wolters (2013) wrote, "the experience of the financial crisis did influence the debates in Central Asia on economic development, mostly towards questions of alternative sources of capital, but also towards new ways to organize difficult economic and social transformation processes. Islamic financing offers an alternative to both, the search for fresh capital and the debate on social development, yet it also confronts the political regimes as well as the societies in the region with challenges the implications of which for now neither are fully understood nor can be properly measured". The new President of Uzbekistan and the Cabinet of Ministers seem to have already understood these challenges since the trend to accelerate the attraction of Islamic capital increased when Sh. Mirziyoyev, who promised to improve the investment climate to attract more foreign investment, became the President. In general, given the size of the Muslim population and the rich spiritual heritage in terms of Islamic culture and traditions, Uzbekistan should have become the center of Islamic Finance in the region of Central Asia and Transcaucasia. However, I. Karimov's extremely authoritarian rule, which was formed in Uzbekistan in the post-Soviet period, did not allow the potential of Islamic Finance and the overall investment potential of the country to realize.

CHAPTER 3.
AZERBAIJAN

Azerbaijan's ambitions in relation to Islamic Finance were "to build a bridge between Asia and the Middle East, as well as between the CIS and the Persian Gulf countries"[1]. But these goals have not been achieved not only at the interregional level, but even at the national level. Despite numerous statements, the Islamic financial market in the Republic of Azerbaijan hasn't been developed. The country lacked serious discussion about the ideas of Islamic economics, and as a result, it failed to develop its own approach to this issue. However, the country has some practice in attracting Islamic capital, so let's try to analyze it and draw conclusions about the future of Islamic Finance in the country. For this purpose, we collected and analyzed the empirical base of more than 100 deals involving Islamic capital in Azerbaijan. a detailed analysis of all deals allowed us to classify Islamic investors and identify the specifics of their investment strategies in the country.

ISLAMIC DEVELOPMENT BANK GROUP

In 1992 Azerbaijan was the first in the post-Soviet Central Asia and Transcaucasia to join the Organization of Islamic Cooperation. In the same year it entered the Islamic Development Bank (IDB). Since then, the country has attracted more than $1.1 bln from the IDB to invest in 66 projects. This is the fourth result after Uzbekistan, Kazakhstan and Turkmenistan (Appendix B). Azerbaijan's share in the IDB's subscribed capital is 0.1%, and the amount paid for this share is $50.9mln.

The main part (more than 85%) of the capital raised from the IDB was used to finance physical infrastructure. Those were primarily projects in water supply and sanitation (over $450 mln), electric power (over $200 mln) and waste processing (about $200 mln). Besides, those included road construction, airport and educational infrastructure, as well as emergency assistance in restoring social infrastructure for the victims of the earthquake in 2000 and forced migrants from Nagorno-Karabakh (Table 3.1).

---

[1] https://www.trend.az/business/economy/2385070.html

Table 3.1. The IDB deals in Azerbaijan

Sector	Number of IDB deals, pcs.	Total investment by the IDB, $ mln	Share in total investment, %
Water supply and sewerage	10	450.3	40.3
Energy	4	217.3	19.4
Waste processing infrastructure	1	197.6	17.7
Finance	18	91.5	8.2
Industry	13	60.8	5.4
Road construction	5	46.5	4.15
Real Estate	2	20	1.8
Agriculture	3	12.5	1.12
Public administration	4	1.2	0.1
Education	3	0.5	0.05
Airport infrastructure	1	0.25	0.025
Emergency assistance to victims and forced migrants	2	19.2	1.7
Total	66	1,118	100

Source: calculation based on Appendix C.

The three largest investment projects for the IDB in Azerbaijan were the Janub Power Plant ($191 mln), a solid waste disposal plant in the village of Balakhani near Baku ($197.6 mln), and a water supply and treatment project in six regions of the country ($200 mln). They together account for more than half of all IDB investments in this country.

The IDB often co-finances projects on Islamic financial principles in a consortium with other international development banks (such as the World Bank, the International Finance Corporation, the Asian Development Bank, the European Bank for Reconstruction and Development, and others). For example, in 2009 it invested in the construction of the *Janub Gas Power Plant* with a capacity of 780MW, which cost about 700 mln euros. The power plant was built on the site of the second-largest Shirvan thermal power plant built in the 1960s. The Asian Development Bank provided guarantees for the project in the amount of 220 mln euros, while the IDB provided Islamic istisna financing in the amount of $191 mln, a consortium of three commercial banks (German Bayerische Landesbank, French Societe Generale and Swiss Credit Suisse) provided syndicated financing in the amount of 285 mln euros under 10-year state guarantees, and the OPEC Fund for International Development — 34 mln euros. According to the documentation, civil works on the construction and commissioning of the power plant building were carried out at the expense of the IDB[1]. The reconstruction of the *Mingechaur Hydro Power Plant*, a similar but smaller project, was funded in 1998. The IDB invested $12.7 mln, the European Bank for Reconstruction and Development — $21.65 mln, and Azenerji and EC Tacis — $10.3 mln.

Due to the IDB's investments, *a waste processing plant* was built in 2010 on the site of a previously existing open landfill near Baku. The total cost of the project was more than $350 mln, of which the IDB allocated $197.6 mln for the purchase of specialized equipment according to the Islamic financial standard istisna for a period of 18 years (including 3-year grace period), and the remaining part was covered by the state budget of Azerbaijan. In 2009 they laid the foundation, and in 2012 the plant was opened. The World Bank provided its recommendations for the project, but failed to provide financial support. The construction, design and management of the plant were entrusted to the CNIM Group, a French industrial contractor, for a 20-year period. The Group had managed 12 similar projects in France and the UK since 1969. The capacity of the Azerbaijani plant is 500,000 tons of household waste per annum. In addition, the plant can burn up to 10,000 tons of hospital waste annually. The incineration process generates 231.5 mln kwh of electricity per annum, which is supplied to the city electric grid to provide energy to 50,000 houses, and the remaining ash and slag is used for asphalt production. The plant allows to save up to 60 mln cubic meters of natural gas annually. It currently employs about 100 people. Before its construction, 80% of all household waste generated in Baku was buried in open disposals, which caused serious environmental threats.

Table 3.1 shows that the biggest IDB investments were in the water supply and sewerage infrastructure of Azerbaijan. Of the 10 projects, we will only focus on one — the reconstruction of the *Samur-Absheron Canal*, which was built in 1939–1940 using the method of folk construction. The total cost of reconstruction of the 29-km section of the canal approximated $50 mln, of which the IDB gave $10.2 mln, the Saudi Fund for Development — $18 mln (for a period of 25 years including a 7-year grace period), the OPEC Fund for International Development — $8 mln, and the government of Azerbaijan — $6.5 mln. Previously, the 37-km section of the canal was built with the loans from the World Bank. The main purpose of the canal is irrigation of arid

---

[1] https://www.adb.org/projects/documents/janub-gas-fired-power-plant-project-rrp

agricultural lands of the Apsheron Peninsula of Azerbaijan, as well as water supply to Baku and Sumgait.

In the road construction sector, the reconstruction project of the 86-km section of the *Yevlakh—Ganja road* connecting Baku with the Georgian border should be analyzed in detail. The total cost of the project, which was implemented in 2007—2008, exceeded $70 mln, of which $52 mln in the form of a loan at 1.5% for a grace period was provided by the Asian Development Bank, $10.1 mln was invested by the IDB, and the Saudi Fund for Development gave $11 mln for 20 years at 2% for a 5-year grace period. The 52-km section of *Yevlakh—Ujar* was reconstructed in the other direction of the highway at the same time. The IDB allocated $22 mln for this road project, the OPEC Fund for International Development — $6 mln, and the government of Azerbaijan — $3 mln. Besides accelerating the socio-economic development of the 6 regions through which the highway passes, the reconstruction of two road sections also allowed to strengthen inter-country integration[1].

In addition to physical infrastructure, the recipients of the IDB capital are the industrial and financial sectors. For example, the IDB invested more than $90 mln to the financial sector. The funds were mainly intended to finance small and medium-sized businesses in the country. Besides, the IDB financed the creation of Islamic financial institutions — *Ansar Leasing* and the *Caspian International Investment Company*, which will be discussed in detail below. They invested $6.2mln in the equity capital of the former and $7 mln of the latter. To prepare the legal framework in the field of Islamic Finance, the IDB has additionally allocated $200,000 in technical assistance to Azerbaijan for the work of international financial law consultants.

The IDB has directly invested more than $60 mln in the industrial sector. Almost all funds were provided under the murabaha standard.

In 2010 at the 35th meeting of the IDB held in Baku, President of Azerbaijan I. Aliyev noted: "The Islamic Development Bank has played an exclusive role in the development of Azerbaijan's economy"[2]. Our analysis confirms these words, but the Azerbaijani authorities, having accepted Islamic investments for the development of the country's physical infrastructure, have not done the main thing — they have not created conditions for the work of Islamic financial structures within the country.

---

[1] https://www.adb.org/projects/35457-013/main#project-pds
[2] https://az.sputniknews.ru/politics/20100623/43449492.html

ISLAMIC BANKS

The first Islamic bank in Azerbaijan was *Kauthar Bank*. The bank was founded in 1996, but in 2001 it started to introduce changes to work on Islamic financial principles. Analysis of the audited financial statements shows that the bank was not large: for example, in 2009 its assets were estimated as $17 mln[1]. The bank was owned by individuals, including non-residents from Japan, Saudi Arabia, and Canada. In 2013–2014 Kauthar Bank was awarded by World Finance and Global Finance as the 'Best Islamic bank in Azerbaijan'. The bank's clients were individuals, small and medium-sized businesses. In 2006 the bank signed a Cooperation Agreement with the IDB. However, despite these achievements, the bank has neither advertised its work, nor made any attempts to make a name.

In 2007 Bahrain International Investment Bank[2] purchased a 49% stake in Azerbaijan's *Amrahbank* for $46.8 mln in order to transform it into an Islamic bank. Amrahbank has been operating on the Azerbaijani market since 1993 and is owned by individuals. "We believe this investment will benefit from the fast economic growth and the recent developments in the banking industry, where Amrahbank can seize the benefits of being a pioneer in the provision of Shariah-compliant financial products and services in Azerbaijan," commented Aabed Al-Zeera, the executive director of the International Investment Bank[3]. Consultants for this deal were international companies such as Deloitte, E&Y, and Baker & McKenzie.

The acquisition of Amrahbank by a Bahraini investor allowed the Azerbaijani bank to establish cooperation with a number of well-known Middle Eastern financial institutions, such as Gulf Finance House, Turkapital Holding and the International Islamic Trade and Finance Corporation of the IDB group (ITFC). In addition, the bank has attracted finance from the Saudi Fund for Development, the OPEC Fund for International Development, and the Islamic Private Sector Development Corporation of the IDB group (ICD). Despite this success, the new owner failed to fully transform Amrahbank into an

---

[1] http://www.kautharbank.com/en/audit/
[2] International Investment Bank was founded as an Islamic bank in 2003 in Bahrain by Middle Eastern investors. Today, the bank has more than 100 shareholders and, in fact, it operates as an Asset Manager, placing its shareholders' funds in various assets, ranging from real estate to private equity funds in the Middle East and Europe. The analysis of the bank's audited reports showed that its most expensive acquisition was the European Islamic Investment Bank (now, Rasmala) in the UK for $67.8 mln in 2005.
[3] https://www.arabnews.com/node/304960

Islamic bank due to lack of proper legislation. Today this Azerbaijani bank still operates as a interest-based financial institution. In 2013 a Bahraini investor initiated a partial exit (sale) from the asset, but as of 2018, the bank was still in the Bahraini investor's portfolio, despite the recommendation of the Shariah Board in the annual report to completely exit the asset[1]. No doubt, the sale of Amrahbank is only a matter of time and the ability to find and negotiate with proper acquirer.

In 2011 URALSIB, previously owned by Russian billionaire N. Tsvetkov, and then, *Nikoil Bank,* taken over by another billionaire V. Alekperov, introduced the Islamic product of wadiah yad dhamanah[2]. Previously, the bank did research and confirmed the demand for this product among the Muslim population of the country who adheres to the norms of Islam. According to the bankers, the product did not contradict the country's legislation and, at the same time, followed all the requirements of Shariah. For this purpose, consultations with Islamic financial organizations: AAOIFI, Islamic Research and Training Institute (IDB group), Amanie Advisors were held in advance. Access to the product had been provided in all 14 branches of the bank in Azerbaijan until 2015, but today it is no longer in the portfolio, so it is almost impossible to assess if it was a great success and in demand among the population.

When working with the corporate sector, Islamic financial standards were used by many conventional Azerbaijani banks that attracted financing from the IDB for the development of small and medium-sized businesses in the country. These were Turan Bank ($13.8 mln), Rabita Bank ($2.6 mln), Unibank ($21.7 mln), Standard Bank ($3 mln), and Azerdemiryol Bank ($3 mln). For such purposes, international development banks provide financing without government guarantees.

At the end of 2010, one of the recipients of capital from the IDB, *Turan Bank* of Azerbaijan, announced its intention to apply Islamic financial standards not only in the corporate but also in the retail sector. In the same year, the IDB also stated, "it is ready to participate in the establishment of an Islamic bank in Azerbaijan, but for this purpose, the Ministry of Economic Development and Finance must first apply with such an initiative"[3]. However, there were no attempts to establish a full-fledged Islamic bank in Azerbaijan, but the initiative to create an Islamic window within the framework of the largest state bank —

---

[1] https://www.iib-bahrain.com/annual-report/
[2] Wadiah yad dhamanah is Islamic financial agreement of safekeeping or guaranteed deposits.
[3] https://www.trend.az/business/economy/1211971.html

the International Bank of Azerbaijan (IBA)[1] was implemented. In 2009 the IBA created a special group for the organization of the Islamic window, and, a year earlier, the bank opened offices in Qatar and Dubai (now shut down). At the same time D.Hajiyev, the former chairman of the IBA board, said, "The creation of a separate structure for Islamic banking in the IBA will allow Azerbaijan to become a regional center for Islamic Finance"[2]. The Islamic window at the IBA was opened in September 2012, but was later transformed into the Department of Islamic banking. a consortium of international consultants: Salans, KPMG, Pinsent Masons and Daral Shariah[3] assisted the bank to create this structure. In 2013 the new department started servicing clients, and its list of services includes Islamic leasing (ijarah), Islamic deposits (waqala), Islamic debit cards and Islamic charity loans (qard-hasan).

In 2014 the IBA was 219th (out of 360 possible) in the ranking of the largest Islamic financial institutions ('Top Islamic Financial Institutions') by The Banker, a British journal. "At the end of 2013, the assets of the Islamic banking department of the bank amounted to $180 mln, which is approximately 1.8% of the total assets of the IBA. At the end of last year net income from the bank's Islamic operations amounted to 7.69% of the bank's total income", the comments to the rating said. In the rating of the journal, which includes only commercial banks, the IBA took the 156th place out of 214 possible ones. The transparency of the banking system in Azerbaijan is low: most Azerbaijani banks, including the IBA, do not publish their financial statements, which prevents making an objective analysis of the bank's performance. But according to the management of this department, the success was very impressive, "within 9 months of 2014, the total volume of deposits of the population in Baku increased almost 10 times: as of January 1 of this year, the total volume of deposits was 1.69 mln manats, by the beginning of October, this figure increased to 10.1 mln manats, and the investment portfolio of the department increased 1.5 times, and amounted to 175.7 mln manats. As of October 2014, the total amount of funds raised from international financial markets was $218.7 mln"[4]; a quote from another interview says that "the IBA's portfolio of Islamic banking amounted to about 172–

---

[1] IBA was founded in 1992 and is the successor of the Azerbaijan branch of Vnesheconombank of the USSR. All the years after its foundation, the bank was the largest in the country and occupied 30–40% of the market.
[2] https://www.trend.az/business/economy/2024448.html
[3] Daral Shariah is a Shariah consulting company established by the oldest Islamic bank, Dubai Islamic Bank.
[4] https://vesti.az/ekonomika/investicionnyj-portfel-departamenta-islamskogo-bankinga-mba-uvelichilsya-v-15-raza-222922

173 mln manats. Of these, about 130 mln manats, where 45% is allocated for mortgage financing, are accounted for by leasing. The remaining 42–43 mln manats are allocated for corporate and consumer financing"[1]. It was planned that by the end of 2014, the IBA would present Islamic banking outside of Baku: the corresponding departments were planned to be opened in Ganja, Lankaran and Sumgait.

The banking market regulator was also satisfied with the results of the pilot project. According to R. Orujev, the former managing director of the Central Bank of Azerbaijan, "currently, 3,500– 4,000 citizens have applied to the IBA for financial resources within the framework of Islamic banking"[2]. At that time, experts estimated the market of Islamic Finance in Azerbaijan, consisting of 7 banks, leasing and microfinance organizations at 300 mln manats or $400 mln[3].

In 2014 the *IBA raised $252 mln in syndicated Islamic funding* from the international consortium of Al Hilal Bank, Barwa Bank, Citigroup, Dubai Islamic Bank, JP Morgan and Noor Bank. In the same year, the bank started its Islamic banking business in Moscow.

At the peak of its popularity, the IBA's Islamic Finance portfolio was $526 mln[4]. "A unique alternative banking model was tested in Azerbaijan, which, without a legal framework, managed to be a success. From servicing retail clients, issuing plastic cards as part of Islamic financing to documentary operations for large corporate clients <...> We were the first to actively finance the retail segment, issued Islamic cards, mortgage products for the retail sector, and financed micro-loans within the framework of Islamic lending", head of the department B. Gurbanzade said at the time[5]. However, despite these results, the IBA's Islamic banking department was closed down in October 2015. In our opinion, it may be at least partially linked to the international banking scandal related to the former Chairman of the IBA Board and his family, as well as the actual announcement of the bank's default on external obligations[6].

Despite further attempts to create Islamic microfinance funds (with Azercredit in 2015 and FINOCO in 2017), a grant from the IDB for the development of legislation, and debates on opening an independent

---

[1] https://news.day.az/economy/556099.html
[2] https://az.sputniknews.ru/economy/20141114/301217593.html
[3] https://ru.oxu.az/economy/64001
[4] https://www.trend.az/business/economy/2379686.html
[5] https://news.day.az/economy/722710.html
[6] See i) https://novayagazeta.ru/articles/2018/11/07/78483-kto-hochet-stat-milliarderom-tot-syadet ii)https://www.reuters.com/article/us-azerbaijan-iba-debt-idUSKBN1880UH

Islamic bank with out-of-office service, this topic gradually faded, and in 2019, the Moody's international rating agency assessed the potential for the development of Islamic banking in Azerbaijan as low. "Without active government interference in the development of the sector, its growth will be limited", the agency's analysts explained[1].

ISLAMIC LEASING (IJARAH) COMPANIES

At the end of 2008 the Islamic Corporation for Private Sector Development of the IDB group (ICD) founded the Islamic leasing company *Ansar Leasing* in Baku (the legal name is Azerbaijan leasing company, LLC). The Islamic investor allocated $6.2 mln in its capital. The authorized capital was expected to reach $50 mln in the future. At that time, Ansar Leasing was considered to be the most capitalized leasing company, while local leasing companies had a critical funding situation. First of all, this was due to the 2008–2009 global financial crisis. Ansar Leasing provides business with Islamic leasing financing for a period of 1–6 years with the initiator's down payment of 20–25% of the project cost. As of mid-2012, Ansar Leasing's leasing portfolio was $15.7 mln. The company's clients were both individuals and businesses. Besides, in 2012 Ansar Leasing was preparing to issue Islamic bonds (sukuk) with a yield of 9–10%, first on the local and then on foreign markets. But that did not happen.

Unileasing had an earlier experience in attracting Islamic leasing financing. This company with an authorized capital of 1.8 mln manats ($2.1 mln) was founded in 2004 by the Azerbaijani UniBank (66.67%) and the European Bank for Reconstruction and Development (33.33%). In 2005, the ICD allocated $1.7 mln to Unileasing as part of the Private Enterprise Development Project. The first deal of Unileasing was the Islamic financing of the purchase of commercial real estate value of 434 th manats. According to the company, to complete this deal, consultations were held with specialists from leading banks in Malaysia. Later, other international development banks started financing this leasing company: the International Finance Corporation ($5 mln in 2006), the European Bank for Reconstruction and Development ($3 mln in 2006), the Export-Import Bank of the United States ($2.5 mln in 2008). At the end of 2011 another company from the IDB group — the International Islamic Trade and Finance Corporation (ITFC) — provided Unileasing with Islamic capital in the amount of $3.5 mln to finance the supply of the products of small and medium-sized businesses.

---

[1]   http://interfax.az/view/774919

The main problem of the leasing market in Azerbaijan is lack of the availability of funds. The companies' small scope of activities and leasing portfolios make this sphere less attractive to all investors, including Islamic ones. This is one of the features of the poorly developed financial market of Azerbaijan, where, according to experts, only 0.5% of fixed assets are purchased via leasing, while in developed countries this figure exceeds 50%[1].

PRIVATE EQUITY FUNDS

In 2008 the *Caspian International Investment LTD* with an initial capital of 2.5 mln manats was established in Baku. Its founders were the state-owned Azerbaijan Investment Company (25%) and the ICD from the IBD group (75%). Then other investors — Al Ahmar (Yemen), Saham Holding (Kuwait) and the IDB — joined the company, and the authorized capital increased to 31 mln manats. Since then, the company's structure has changed as follows: Azerbaijan Investment Company owns 24% of the shares, the IDB — 28%, Hameed Abdullah Hussein Al-Ahmar — 16%, Saham Holding — 14%, the ICD — 18%. Thus, the IDB directly and indirectly owns 42% of the shares of this investment company.

The Caspian International Investment LTD is an Islamic financial company. This is confirmed by marketing materials, and by the annual audited reports, where one of the items of expenditure is the Shariah advisory fee accruals (accrued expenses for Shariah consulting services). At the same time, it is surprising that in different years, the company placed from 10 to 60% of its assets on deposits in banks at an effective interest rate of 3 to 9%[2].

In our opinion, the establishment of such an investment company before the creation of the above-mentioned Department of Islamic banking in the IBA is a kind of compromise between the IDB and the Azerbaijani authorities. The statement made by R. Aslanli, the Chairman of the State Committee on Securities of Azerbaijan, in 2010, confirms that "there is no great need in Azerbaijan to introduce Islamic banking in the country's banking sector <...> but if Islamic instruments are introduced through investment funds and this is within the framework of legislation, we do not intend to pay attention to the religious affiliation of investors"[3]. At the same time R. Melikova, the Director of the Legal

---

[1] https://az.sputniknews.ru/economy/20120403/297116041.html
[2] https://ciic.az/media-annual-reports/
[3] https://www.trend.az/business/economy/1707246.html

department of the Central Bank of Azerbaijan, said, "today, these [Islamic banks] are not a priority of our activities. Azerbaijan is a secular state, and, in fact, the rules that are applied in the classical banking sector satisfy many individuals, legal entities and officials".

According to its strategy, the Caspian International Investment LTD invests in accordance with Islamic financial principles in the real economy, with the exception of oil and gas production, conventional banks and insurance companies. The company provides investment projects with equity financing, which, unlike conventional banking, does not have fixed credit payments. Two Shariah standards are used for this purpose: musharaka and mudaraba. In both cases, funds are provided for 3–5 years with a minimum expected return of 20–25%. According to the official website, when co-financing the project with its initiator (musharaka), the Caspian International Investment LTD can provide 1–5 mln manats, and, when the initiator acts as a project manager and does not invest its own funds — only 200–500 manats.

The Caspian International Investment LTD has invested in 8 projects in the fields of agriculture (Our Orchards, Agroterm, T-Tomatoes, A-Agro), logistics (Agro-Trading, Agrotara), real estate (Imara) and industry (A-Plastic). The analysis of the company's financial statements shows that the company's revenue was mainly generated through the sale of agricultural products.

Despite its name, in fact, Caspian International Investment LTD is a joint investment fund. Several other similar funds were initiated: the Kuwait-Azerbaijan Company (a joint fund of Azerbaijan Investment Company (25%) and Turkapital, a subsidiary of Kuwait Finance House (75%)), the Emirati-Azerbaijan Fund (2009), and Qatar-Azerbaijan Fund (2017). However, the first company was liquidated soon after its creation, and the second and third companies remained in the status of 'intentions'.

Thus, having collected and analyzed a database of more than 100 deals involving Islamic capital in Azerbaijan, we estimate its total volume at more than $1.7 bln. Most of this capital is the IDB investment. This figure could be much higher, and the investment structure would include private Islamic capital, if the country created conditions ('rules of the game'), at least consisting of special legislation required for the full operation of business on Islamic financial principles. This is the first and important limiting factor in the development of this industry in the country. According to the Chairman of the Board of the private local Islamic bank of Azerbaijan — Kauthar Bank, in fact, the only one in

Azerbaijan, — the second factor is lack of sufficient financial resources (essentially, liquidity) for development (Bekkin, 2009). This requires either attracting a large investor or developing Islamic capital markets, for example, through the issue of Islamic bonds (sukuk).

Islamic banks, Islamic financial organizations (insurance and leasing companies, asset managers, funds) and Islamic capital markets are able to occupy a significant niche in the Azerbaijani market. Moreover, our analysis of deals not only confirms demand for that among businesses and the population, but also indicates a rich practice of attracting Islamic capital in both domestic and foreign markets. However, as R. Bekkin (2009) noted in his work, "implementing the principles of secularism, Azerbaijani officials automatically oppose any projects at the state level if the word 'Islamic' is mentioned, even if we are talking about such a phenomenon as Islamic Finance and Islamic banks in particular". Moreover, the desire to protect themselves from potential political risks regularly forces local authorities to suppress any form of social and economic innovation. Therefore, the future of Islamic Finance in the country remains unclear. The Economist's forecasts confirm that: "The banking sector will remain underdeveloped in the medium term owing to the government's lack of a comprehensive reform strategy <...> Significant institutional change is unlikely, owing to the authoritarian political system, the overlap of corporate and political interests, and the highly concentrated ownership structure of the economy"[1].

---

[1] https://eiu.bvdep.com

CHAPTER 4.
TURKMENISTAN

"A dictatorship and one of the most secret, closed and authoritarian countries in the world", this is how Turkmenistan is described by the Economist in its country outlook[1]. It was the authoritarian regime that led to the economy, which is characterized by the dominance of state monopolies and over-concentration of exports on narrow range of commodities.

In terms of nominal GDP, Turkmenistan is the second largest economy after Kazakhstan in post-Soviet Central Asia and Transcaucasia. According to the Asian Development Bank, half of its structure is formed by revenues from the sale of mineral resources, namely, natural gas (ADB, 2017). According to the Central Intelligence Agency, Turkmenistan is ranked 5th in the world in terms of proven gas reserves and 10th in terms of gas exports. Russia, Iran, Qatar, and Saudi Arabia only have the largest gas reserves[2]. Turkmenistan's main export trading partner is China, where more than 80% of all exported gas is supplied. Besides natural gas, the country exports petroleum products, peat and cotton. The country's import is more diversified: Turkey accounts for 20% of total import, China — 13%, Russia — 12%, UAE — 11%, and Germany — 7% (Appendix A). The country imports machinery and equipment, metal pipes, and chemical products (mainly medicines and fertilizers). In general, the economy of this country, being a commodity-rich economy, is highly dependent on the situation in the commodity markets. Thus, the fall in natural gas prices immediately affects the country's economic growth rate, as can be clearly seen in Fig.4.1.

Due to intensive production and export of natural gas, the country's wealth, measured in GDP per capita at purchasing power parity, increased 4-fold in 1995–2019: from $3,099 to $12,410. At the end of 2019 this was the third result in the Central Asia and Transcaucasia after Kazakhstan ($28,510) and Azerbaijan ($18,660). The economies of all the three countries are commodity-based ones. Over the same period the population of Turkmenistan increased by 40%: from 4.2 mln in 1994 to 5.9 mln in 2019.

---

[1] https://eiu.bvdep.com
[2] https://www.cia.gov/library/publications/resources/the-world-factbook/

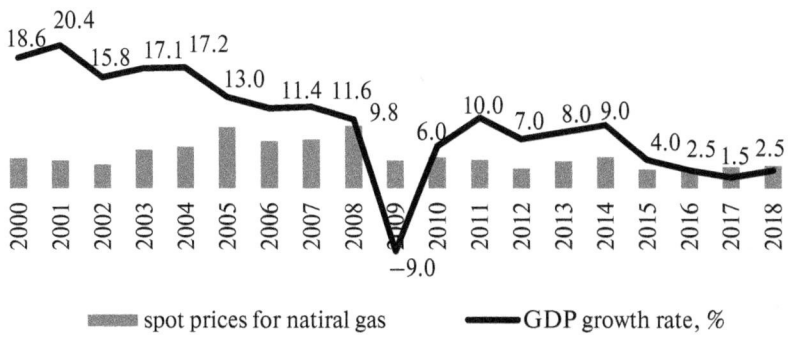

20.4
18.6 15.8 17.1 17.2
           13.0 11.4 11.6
                      9.8
                         6.0 10.0 7.0 8.0 9.0
                                              4.0 2.5 1.5 2.5
−9.0

2000 2001 2002 2003 2004 2005 2006 2007 2008 2009 2010 2011 2012 2013 2014 2015 2016 2017 2018

▬ spot prices for natiral gas   ▬GDP growth rate, %

Fig. 4.1. Spot prices for natural gas and GDP growth rates in Turkmenistan.
Source: the Economist Intelligence Unit[1] and U.S. Energy Information Administration[2].

In fact, Turkmenistan lacks environment for private investors to conduct business. The reasons for this are state control in all economic spheres, non-compliance with the law and a high level of corruption[3]. Therefore, foreign direct investment is directed only to political and highly profitable commodity projects financed by loans from international development banks. This was the case, for example, in late 1999, when the European Bank for Reconstruction and Development granted an 8-year loan totaling $75 mln to Dragon Oil, a company owned by the UAE government (through Emirates National Oil Company). The funds raised were used for oil and gas development on the Caspian shelf. Since 1996 Petronas, a company owned by the government of Malaysia, has been operating four gas, oil and gas condensate production platforms in the Turkmen part of the Caspian sea. In 2019 this Malaysian company extended the production sharing agreement with the government of Turkmenistan until 2038[4].

Despite Turkmenistan's so-called "official policy of neutrality"[1], the country is a member of various multilateral organizations. Thus, in 1992 Turkmenistan, along with other young Central Asian states, became a member of the Organization of Islamic Cooperation, and, in 1994,

---

[1] https://eiu.bvdep.com
[2] https://www.eia.gov/dnav/ng/hist/rngwhhdA.htm
[3] In terms of the corruption perception level, Turkmenistan is on the 165th place (out of 180 possible) in the world. The situation is slightly better in other post-Soviet countries: Kazakhstan ranks 113th, Azerbaijan — 126th, and Russia — 137th (Transparency International, 2019).
[4] https://www.nst.com.my/news/nation/2019/10/533769/dr-m-turkmenistan-extend-petronas-psc-2038

Table 4.1. The IDB deals in Turkmenistan

Sector	Number of the IDB deals, pcs.	Total investment by the IDB, $ mln	Share in total investment, %
Oil and gas transportation	3	742	51.19
Railway infrastructure	2	388	26.77
Telecommunication	2	288.1	19.88
Healthcare	4	30.2	2.08
Education	1	0.3	0.02
Road infrastructure	1	0.3	0.02
Water supply and irrigation	1	0.3	0.02
Energy	1	0.2	0.01
Total	15	1,449.4	100

Source: calculation based on Appendix C.

joined the Islamic Development Bank (IDB). The country's share in the subscribed capital of this multilateral development bank is 0.01%, the amount contributed is almost $5 mln (Appendix B).

To date, the IDB has financed 15 projects in Turkmenistan totaling $1.45 bln (Table 4.1). In terms of value, this is the third result in the region after Uzbekistan and Kazakhstan (Appendix B). However, it is the last result in terms of the number of projects. Analysis of the IDB deals shows that even in such small economies as Kyrgyzstan and Tajikistan, the IDB has implemented 50–60 projects for a much smaller investment. Thus, in Turkmenistan the average size of one deal is $96.6 mln. This is the highest value for the post-Soviet countries.

So, according to the content analysis of Turkmen deals, half of all investments attracted from the IDB fall on one project — the construction of the *TAPI Gas Pipeline* connecting Turkmenistan, Afghanistan, Pakistan and India. As of 2008, the cost of the project with a length of more than 1,800 km and a capacity of 33bln cubic meters of gas was estimated at $7.6 bln. The gas pipeline comes from one of the largest gas and oil fields in the world — Galkynysh. Since 2003 the TAPI Secretariat has been another multilateral development bank — the Asian Development Bank (ADB). Turkmenistan joined it in 2000. The leader of the consortium for the construction, financing and operation of the pipeline is Turkmengaz. It owns 85% of the project. Despite the fact that the construction of the TAPI began in late 2015, its history goes back to 1995, when Turkmenistan and Pakistan, with the diplomatic support of the United States, signed a Letter of Intent on the primary version of the Turkmenistan–Pakistan gas pipeline. Then the project began to expand: in 2002, in Islamabad, the heads of Turkmenistan, Afghanistan, Pakistan and India officially announced the launch of the updated project. That meeting established a project steering committee consisting of the energy ministers of the participating countries, and the ADB was appointed as the leading development partner. The project was periodically suspended as the situation in Afghanistan was getting worse. To this day, the geopolitical risk associated with the destabilization of the political situation in Afghanistan remains the main problem of the project. Despite this, in 2012 the ADB provided technical assistance in the amount of $1.5 mln, which included costs for the analytical and organizational parts of the project. To date, the share of Turkmengaz in the consortium is 85%, Pakistan's Inter State Gas Systems — 5%, India's GAIL — 5% and Afghan Gas Enterprise — 5%.

Despite the world's largest gas reserves, Turkmenistan has access to only three markets — China, Iran and Russia. In the case of Russia, due to its monopoly position, Gazprom either completely stops buying Turkmen gas or starts buying it again. In the case of Iran, the Turkmen authorities themselves cut off gas supplies because of debts. Fuel supplies to China are made to repay the company's loan, which is estimated at least $8 bln[1]. Thus, Turkmenistan was forced to develop new markets and the TAPI became one of the key projects for the country. The agreement on the implementation of the TAPI was signed in Washington at a session of the International Monetary Fund and the World Bank. Later, head of the state G. Berdimuhamedov offered Malaysia, Qatar, Saudi Arabia, and Germany to share in the capital of the project's roadshow. In 2016 he attracted funding from the IDB in the amount of $700 mln. However, we do not know on what terms the funds were raised. According to the ADB documents, the TAPI is intended to reduce the electricity deficit in Afghanistan, Pakistan and India: Turkmen gas is supposed to be used for power generation instead of coal. This will reduce harmful emissions into the atmosphere by 43% (ADB, 2012). This pipeline, passing through southern Afghanistan, should provide new jobs during its construction and operation, as well as create favorable conditions for the development of the industrial potential of this territory. In February 2018 the Afghan section of the TAPI Gas Pipeline was launched officially, and the pipeline is planned to be fully commissioned in 2020. In addition to this large-scale project, the IDB has twice financed the *purchase of oil tankers* for a total of $42 mln. The deal was implemented in the form of Islamic

---

[1] https://www.bbc.com/news/business-30131418

leasing (ijarah). These tankers transport oil produced in the Caspian sea by the aforementioned Dragon Oil (UAE) to Azerbaijan and Russia.

In 2007 Turkmenistan signed a multilateral agreement with neighboring countries on the development of the *North-South railway corridor*. The goals of the project were to increase the volume of regional trade and further integration. Besides enhancing trade between Iran and Kazakhstan, the North-South Railway was also supposed to improve Turkmenistan's connection with the markets of Kazakhstan and the Russian Federation, the Persian Gulf and South Asia countries. Connecting Uzen (Kazakhstan) in the North and Gorgan (Iran) in the South, the corridor passes through the territory of Turkmenistan. 724 km of railway tracks were built here: the 467-km Northern section of the railway was built by the government of Turkmenistan with its own funds and the ADB's loan of $125 mln, and the remaining 257-km (Southern) section with 69 km of auxiliary tracks connecting the Turkmen Bereket and the Iranian Gorgan was financed by the IDB and the government of Turkmenistan. In 2010 the IDB allocated $388 mln in two tranches to the project. The railway passes through the territory of the strategic region of Turkmenistan — the Balkan Velayat, where large deposits of oil, gas, coal, platinum, gold, uranium and semiprecious stones are concentrated. The railway will allow Turkmenistan to increase the supply of these goods to neighboring countries. However, despite the implementation of large-scale transport projects, the infrastructure of Turkmenistan remains underdeveloped, and logistics costs are quite high: according to the Logistics Performance Index developed by the World Bank, Turkmenistan is almost at the very end of the list: on the 142nd place out of 167 possible[1].

In the *telecommunication sector* of Turkmenistan the IDB financed two projects totaling $288 mln. It should be noted that Turkmenistan lacks free access to the Internet. Local authorities periodically block access to social networks, messengers, and alternative sources of information. Moreover, there are elements of the cult of personality of the head of the state[2]. In general, these are the negative aspects of an authoritarian regime characterized by centralization and unpredictability, which caused MTS, a Russian telecommunication company, to leave the market at the end of 2017. Today, there are no private or international telecommunication operators in the country. State monopolies only operate here — Turkmentelecom (fixed-line communications) and Altyn Asyr (mobile

---

[1] https://lpi.worldbank.org/international/aggregated-ranking
[2] https://carnegie.ru/commentary/77380

communications). At the end of 2017 the government of Turkmenistan received $273 mln from the IDB for their development. The funds raised will be used to build 5G networks, a data center, and so on.

The IDB allocated more than $30 mln for the development of *healthcare* in Turkmenistan, more than $9 mln of which was invested in the development of a water resort founded in Archman in 1925. The funds were allocated for 7 years, the resort reconstruction project was implemented by an Emirati company, and the equipment was upgraded by Siemens, a well-known German company. The funds allocated by the IDB were repaid from the State Health Development Fund of Turkmenistan. In addition, five diagnostic centers were built in various regions of country with the IDB's investment of more than $15 mln.

As shown in Table 4.1, four small projects totaling $1.1 mln were funded by the IDB. They included a few educational projects: an Islamic institute and four madrasaas ($305,000); and feasibility studies for the construction of the Turkmenbashi–Karabogaz Road ($275,000), the Kazandzhik–Kyzylatrek Irrigation Canal ($263,219), and the production of solar panels of Karakum sand ($189,684). The later projects have not resulted in further investment from the IDB.

Thus, the investment strategy of the IDB in Turkmenistan is only focused on two infrastructure sectors — oil and gas transportation and railway construction, which together account for almost three-quarters of all investments (more than 70%). On the one hand, these projects are political, on the other hand, they are of an important cross-border nature and are aimed at interregional integration of the country outside the post-Soviet area. At the same time, if they are successfully implemented, they should help Turkmenistan get out of economic isolation.

In general, the IDB does not actually conduct active investment activities in Turkmenistan. It is limited to financing medical projects (subject to their implementation by foreign contractors). There was the only exception — short-term financing of the telecommunication infrastructure after the Russian investor (MTS) left the market. Turkmenistan does not encourage any private initiative, so the IDB is not able to finance either the industrial, or financial, or agricultural sectors, like, for example, in neighboring countries. The attempts by the IDB and its subsidiaries to sign agreements with the Turkmen authorities failed. The country lacks Islamic banks and other Islamic financial institutions that could become conduits of Islamic capital to the local population. This seriously limits the potential and future of Islamic Finance in Turkmenistan.

CHAPTER 5.
KYRGYZSTAN

Kyrgyzstan is one of the poorest countries in the post-Soviet region with GDP per capita almost seven times lower than in Russia ($4,220 against $28,120). One fifth of the country's population (19.1%) lives below the poverty line. Almost a third of the country's economy (29%) is represented by remittances from Russia and Kazakhstan. Gold mining actually represented by an only company Kumtor forms 9% of GDP and 37% of the country's exports (IMF, 2019a). Trade accounts for 20% of the economy, while agriculture accounts for 14%. The population of Kyrgyzstan as a whole is poorly urbanized since two-thirds of it lives in rural areas. What is more, 40% of the rural population of the Republic have no access to clean drinking water.

However, it should be recognized that unlike a number of other post-Soviet Central Asian and Transcaucasian countries, the private sector plays a major role in the Kyrgyz economy, which, according to the EBRD (2018) estimates, generates 70–75% of GDP, while small and medium-sized businesses account for up to 40% of GDP. At the same time, EBRD analysts shows that local private businesses cannot boast high productivity and competitiveness. There are many reasons for this, e.g. lack of adequate public infrastructure and reliable access to electricity. Low availability of funding is yet another aggravating factor. Banks prefer to focus on the urban population and lend to large enterprises, invoking lack of collateral with small and medium-sized businesses. In this regard, a growing role is played by alternative sources and ways of financing. Of particular interest for this study is Islamic capital which was institutionalized in Kyrgyzstan in 2006, earlier than in all other post-Soviet countries. To do this, we identified and analyzed about 80 deals, which allowed us to identify and classify the most active participants in the investment process. We also tried to understand the logic of their decisions and, ultimately, determine the specifics of their investment strategies in the Kyrgyz Republic.

ISLAMIC DEVELOPMENT BANK GROUP

After gaining sovereignty, Kyrgyzstan joined the Organization of the Islamic Conference (now the Organization of Islamic Cooperation) along with other CIS countries with a predominantly Muslim population in 1992. In 1993, the Republic became a member of the Islamic Development Bank (IDB), the main multilateral development Bank under this organization.

Our analysis showed that since 1993, Kyrgyzstan has attracted more than $0.3 bln in investment from this bank for the implementation of 50 projects. We estimate the average size of an IDB transaction in Kyrgyzstan at $6.5 mln whereas the country's share in the Bank's subscribed capital is 0.05% ($25.8 mln).

We found that more than 90% of the financing attracted to Kyrgyzstan from the IDB, as shown in Table 5.1, was directed to three sectors: energy, road construction and water supply. Besides that, the Bank invested in agriculture, health, finance, education, and public administration, and provided emergency assistance to victims of the Suusamyr earthquake (1992) and the Kyrgyz-Uzbek conflict in Osh (2010).

The largest investment projects in Kyrgyzstan for the IDB were the *CASA-1000 international energy project* which is designed to transfer 1,300 MW of electricity from Kyrgyzstan and Tajikistan to Pakistan and Afghanistan via high–voltage transmission lines with a length of more than 1,200 km (the investment amount was more than $46 mln), and *the reconstruction of the Taraz–Talas–Suusamyr highway* with a total length of 199 km, connecting Kazakhstan with the center of Kyrgyzstan (more than $33 mln) accounting together for a quarter of all IDB investments in the Republic.

Table 5.1. IDB deals in Kyrgyzstan

Sector	Number of IDB deals, pcs.	Total investment by the IDB, $ mln	Share in total investment, %
Energy	7	116	35.8
Road construction	10	108.4	33.5
Water supply and irrigation	6	73	22.6
Agriculture (including microfinancing the rural population)	12	16.2	5.0
Healthcare	2	5	1.5
Emergency assistance to victims	4	3.5	1.1
Finance	4	0.8	0.2
Education	3	0.4	0.1
Public administration	2	0.4	0.1
Total	50	323.7	99.9

Source: calculation based on Appendix C.

We conducted a detailed analysis of each of the IDB's deals in Kyrgyzstan based on all publicly available information including participants, investors, the volume and terms of financing provided. Without underestimating the importance of each of these deals for the society and economy of the Republic we will refrain from discussing them in detail here, presenting only the conclusions of the patterns we found:

- *first,* the IDB provides Kyrgyzstan with preferential long-term financing for up to a 25−30 year period, including 5−10 year grace period, while the rate of return for covering the bank's administrative expenses is 0.75−2.5% per annum;
- *second,* the IDB often participates in deals in a consortium with other international development banks: the World Bank, the Asian Development Bank, the European Bank for Reconstruction and Development, and others;
- *third,* the IDB engages other members of The Arab Coordination Group in its Kyrgyz deals: the Saudi Fund for Development, the OPEC Fund for International Development, the Abu Dhabi Fund for Development, and the Kuwait Fund for Arab Economic Development. This allows: i) to diversify risks, ii) to rise funding in sufficient volume for the implementation of the project, and iii) to establish bilateral investment cooperation between the countries. It is noteworthy that the Saudi Fund for Development invests larger amounts of capital in comparison with other members of the Group;
- *fourth,* the IDB provide capital only on the condition of co-financing by the local government of the Republic, at least in the form of tax benefits for projects implemented;
- *fifth,* despite the implementation of a number of major projects, such as micro-financing of rural residents, the main part of the IDB's investments is directed to financing the physical infrastructure of energy, road construction, water supply, etc.;
- *sixth,* the IDB allocated about $0.8 mln in grants and technical assistance to develop the institutional environment of Islamic Finance in Kyrgyzstan;
- *seventh,* the IDB does not pursue an aggressive financial policy in the Republic, as does, for example, the Export-Import Bank of China. Even with other members of the Arab Coordination Group, the IDB and partners account for 3.4% of the country's total external debt (Fig. 5.1).

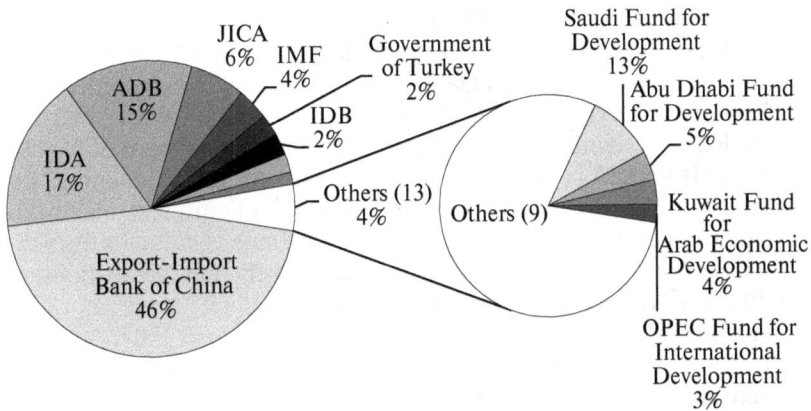

Fig. 5.1. Structure of Kyrgyzstan's public debt at the end of 2019.
Note: IDA stands for International Development Association, and
JICA stands for Japan International Cooperation Agency.
Source: complied according to the Ministry of Finance
of the Kyrgyz Republic[1]

ISLAMIC BANKS

Before turning to Islamic banks, we should pay a little more attention to the current state and problems of the country's banking system. There are more than 20 banks operating in Kyrgyzstan, and despite the structural changes in the market, their number has always remained virtually unchanged. According to the IMF (2019a), the concentration of the banking system in the country can be considered moderate, since the four largest banks account for less than 50% of total assets. Kyrgyzstan's banking system is predominantly private, with foreign ownership accounting for 35% of assets. Local banks, unlike those in Kazakhstan, did not pursue an aggressive policy of external borrowing, and their deposit portfolio has always exceeded the credit one. However, the spread between the interest rate on loans and deposits in Kyrgyzstan is one of the highest in the world due to the low level of competition, large information asymmetry, and high credit risks. In general, the IMF (2019a) survey showed that for 40–50% of small and medium-sized businesses bank financing is almost inaccessible due to their excessively high collateral requirements.

The introduction of Islamic principles of finance in Kyrgyz banking began in 2006. Then, with the financial support of the IDB (the grant

---

[1] http://www.minfin.kg/ru/novosti/mamlekettik-karyz/tyshky-karyz

amount was $255,000), a pilot project was launched on the basis of EcoBank, one of the country's commercial banks. At that time, the new owner of EcoBank, Sh.Martazaliev[1], being personally acquainted with the President of Kyrgyzstan, K. Bakiyev, using the example of Malaysia, succeeded in convincing him of the prospects of the concept of Islamic Finance. It should be noted that until 2006, the development of the Islamic financial direction in the bank was very difficult, and, according to some sources, the bank's management even "received threats from the authorities"[2]. But the situation was changed by the new socio-political conditions in the country: the Tulip revolution.

The official opening of the pilot project took place in 2007. Actually, by form it was an Islamic window which was transformed into a full-fledged Islamic bank by 2016. As the activities of the Islamic window developed, it became clear that the bank should invest in education in order to further develop this area, so in 2008 the Barakat educational center was established to fill this gap. It was here that Tajik bankers and officials who later introduced Islamic principles of finance in their Republic improved their skills[3]. In 2010, the bank finally stopped accepting conventional interest-bearing deposits, transferring its clients (a significant part of them were of Russian ethnic origin) to their Islamic counterparts, and was renamed into *EcoIslamicBank*. One of the bank's press releases stated that 20% of its clients are not Muslims, which generally reflects the global trend in the structure of the client base of Islamic banks. In terms of assets EcoIslamicBank is included in the second ten out of twenty Kyrgyz banks, and according to official data serves more than 100 thousand clients in 100 offices across the country every month. Along with the local experts, the Bank's Shariah Board[4] is also represented by international scholars: e.g., Professor Muhammad Akram bin Laldin, the rector of the Malaysian International Shariah Research Academy for Islamic Finance, member of 16 Shariah boards around the world. Some time later he became Chairman of the Shariah Board of Tawhidbank, the first Islamic Bank in neighboring Tajikistan.

An analysis of the bank's audited financial statements for 2007–2018 showed that in the first year of the pilot project, it only provided funding according to Islamic principles, and in the second year it started accepting deposits as well. With the exception of the first two years of operation, funds raised under Islamic financial principles were always higher than

---

[1] Until 1997, the Bank existed as a joint Kyrgyz-Russian enterprise Russian credit.
[2] https://inosmi.ru/middle_asia/20110621/170979876.html
[3] Tajikistan will be discussed in the next Chapter.
[4] Shariah Board is an independent body which confirms that operations comply with Islamic financing principles.

those provided under the same principles. In addition, the funds raised grew at a faster pace than those provided, but their peak occurred in 2014. It turns out that over all the years of the Islamic financial sector's existence, the bank has attracted more than 20 bln som, and placed more than 9 bln som according to Islamic financial principles (Fig. 5.2).

While in the first year of operation, the Islamic branch of the Bank was unprofitable, in the second year it made a profit: the bank's net income on Islamic financial operations amounted to almost 17 mln soms (in 2018, this figure increased by more than 10 times and amounted to 182 mln soms) (Fig. 5.3).

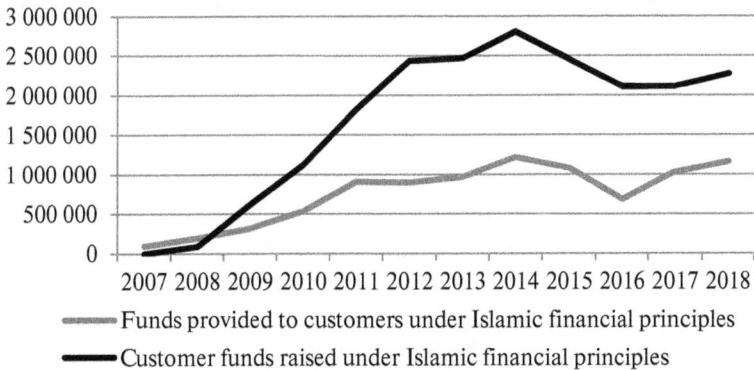

Fig. 5.2. Funds provided and raised under principles of Islamic Finance

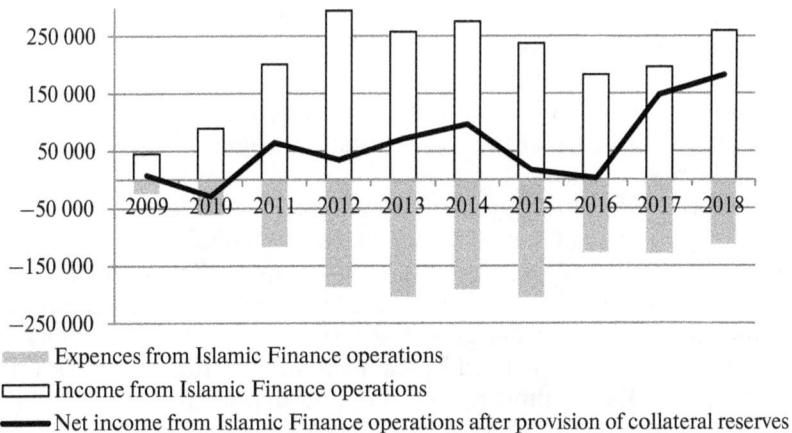

Fig. 5.3. Income, expenses, and net income (after the provision of collateral) from Islamic financial operations

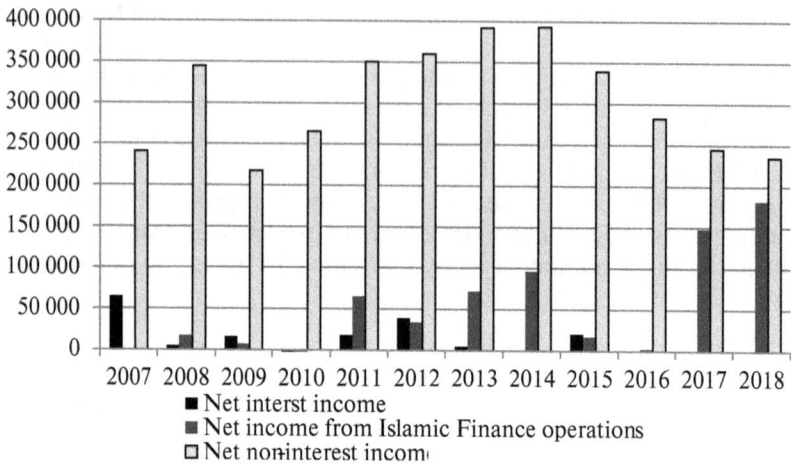

400 000											
350 000											
300 000											
250 000											
200 000											
150 000											
100 000											
50 000											
0											

2007 2008 2009 2010 2011 2012 2013 2014 2015 2016 2017 2018

■ Net interst income
■ Net income from Islamic Finance operations
□ Net non-interest incom

Fig. 5.4. Net interest, non-interest and Islamic Finance income.
Source: compiled from annual audited reports of EcoIslamicBank[1].

However, when analyzing the profitability of the bank's Islamic financial direction, we should be taken into account that in addition to the interest-based income according to Islamic principles, it receives a significant non-interest income, which in the case of EcoIslamicBank in different years amounted from 50 to 100% of the Bank's total operating income. Non-interest income, along with other items, includes profit margin as well as fees for services and commissions on Islamic financial transactions[2]. However, in the case of EcoIslamicBank, we cannot clearly say what the share of Islamic financial operations in the total non-interest income of the bank amounted to. Auditors identified this item only once in 2010. At that time it amounted to 166 mln som, which corresponded to 63% of the bank's total non-interest income for that year (Fig. 5.4).

As for the product line, EcoIslamicBank provides financing for murabaha instead of conventional loans, mudaraba and musharaka instead of interest-bearing deposits, qard-hasan, wadiah yad dhamanah instead of current accounts, and kafala instead of guarantees. The profitability of Islamic deposits is determined by the profitability of commercial projects financed by the bank under principles of Islamic Finance. The Bank's press releases indicate that in 2010 this yield was

---

[1] https://eib.kg/finreport/year.html
[2] Non-interest income of the bank may also include income from deals involving purchase and sale of foreign currency, securities, Islamic derivatives, etc.

in the range from 3 to 17%, depending on the terms and the size of the invested money[1].

During 2018, two new Islamic windows were opened in Kyrgyzstan at Bakai Bank and BTA Bank. The Islamic window at Bakai Bank was called *'The Islamic Financial Center'*. The Center started its development with the simplest and most popular Islamic product — murabaha — which is used to purchase household appliances, furniture, cars, apartments, construction materials, as well as financing the working capital of businesses. This Islamic window allows investors to open qard-hasan demand deposit accounts or mudaraba investment deposits. In the latter case, the clients deposit their money for a certain period and participate in the profit and loss of the Center in a proportion that depends on the amount and terms of the deposit.

In 2019 'The Islamic Financial Center' reported high interest in the Islamic window of Bakai Bank among the population, so an additional center was opened in Osh, the second largest city of Kyrgyzstan. In one interview, the head of this center said: "It is no use expecting someone to come from the outside and bring you money. In fact, there is no miracle, and we must develop ourselves, decide for ourselves what we need and promote it. We already see that the load on the Bakai Bank call center has more questions on Islamic banking than on conventional banking"[2].

The second Bank that opened a similar Islamic window in the same year is *BTA Bank*, formerly owned by the same-named Kazakh bank. In 2019, Bakai Bank and BTA Bank announced their merger. The further strategy was also clarified: "having introduced the innovations, the United Bank will be able to 'look' towards the stock market more often and try issuing bonds, mortgage bonds, and Islamic securities"[3]. In early 2020, BTA Bank finally joined Bakai Bank and started working under its brand. After the merger of the banks, their Islamic windows were also united, expanding the geography of their presence in the cities of Karakol, Tokmak, Kara-Balta and Kyzyl-Kiya. The analysis of the bank's audited financial statements for 2018–2019 shows that over the past year, the funds provided and raised under Islamic principles have more than tripled. Although the net income from Islamic Finance operations accounts for only 14% of the interest income of Bakai Bank, the share of funds provided and raised under Islamic financial principles

---

[1] http://www.tazabek.kg/news:656795/?f=cp
[2] http://ub.kg/ru/banking-novogo-urovnya-v-bishkeke-otkryt-islamskij-finansovyj-tsentr-bakaj-banka/
[3] https://bakai.kg/kg/news/maskarbekova-peremenyi-v-bakaj-banke-i-bta-banke-mogut-privlech-krupnyih-zarubezhnyih-investorov/

45.4% 49.6%

1.8% 4.1%

52.9% 46.3%

12.6% 15.9%

0.5% 1.2%

86.9% 82.8%

2018 2019

2018 2019

- Other
- Funds provided unfer Islamic financial principles
- Credits

- Other
- Funds raised unfer Islamic fiancial principles
- Deposits

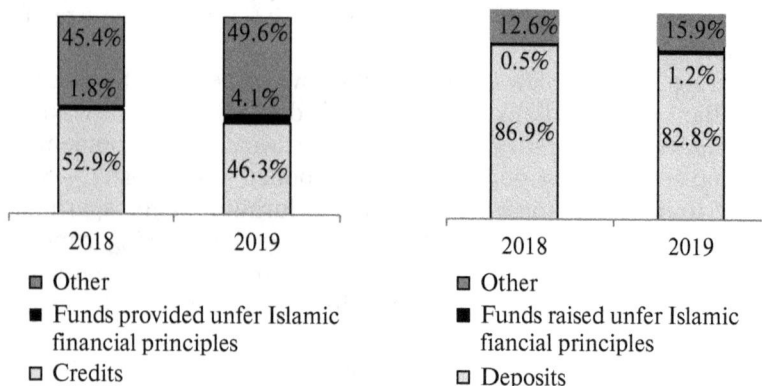

Fig. 5.5. Structure of the Bank's assets and liabilities.
Source: compiled from annual audited reports of Bakai Bank.

morc than doubled in 2019: from 1.8 to 4.1% and from 0.5 to 1.2%, respectively (Fig. 5.5). At the same time, the share of funds provided to clients according to Islamic principles makes 9% of the funds provided at interest rates, while the share of Islamic deposits is 1.6% of the bank's conventional deposits.

At the end of 2019 in Bahrain, Bakai Bank is known to have been negotiating to fund its Islamic window with the headquarters of one of the world's largest Islamic banking structures — Al Baraka Banking Group[1].

Another example: in 2018 the National Bank and the IDB were looking for a partner to create a new Islamic Bank. It also was supposed to act as the co-investors. The partner was required to have managerial and technical experience and was expected to develop policies, procedures and IT systems for the effective functioning of the Islamic Bank. Namely, the National Bank and the IDB planned to act as shareholders of the project without active participation in the day-to-day management of the Bank. The capital of the Islamic Bank was to be $25 mln, equity IRR — 22–38%[2]. However, the IMF gave a negative opinion on such a project, as they foresaw a conflict of interest on the part of the National Bank.

---

[1] https://economist.kg/2019/12/16/islamskij-finansovyj-centr-bta-banka-vstretilsya-s-bahrejnskimi-investorami/
[2] https://eadaily.com/ru/news/2018/07/24/v-kirgizii-sozdayut-pervyy-islamskiy-bank-s-kapitalom-25-mln

Also, in 2018 the government of Kyrgyzstan invited the state-owned Kuwait Finance House to participate in the founding of an Islamic bank. In early 2019 the president of the country already announced that he was expecting proposals to create a new bank in Kyrgyzstan that would work under Islamic principles. In early 2020, the head of the National Bank T. Abdygulov held a meeting with the Director of Abu Dhabi Islamic Bank H. Al-Shamsi, where he discussed opening a subsidiary bank in Kyrgyzstan.

According to the National Bank of Kyrgyzstan, as of June 1, 2017, the share of assets that comply with the Islamic principles was 1.6%, and the most popular product of Islamic banking was murabaha. Besides this, our analysis showed that two of the country's twenty-three banks that develop Islamic financing principles are private. EcoIslamicBank included in the top ten banks in terms of assets (more than 3.2 bln som, or $40 mln as of 2018) is a full-fledged Islamic bank. The second one, BTA Bank, which is one of the top 5 largest banks in Kyrgyzstan with assets of more than $6.3 bln (or $79 mln for 2019), is developing an Islamic financial direction in the format of an Islamic window.

ISLAMIC MICROFINANCE COMPANIES

According to the EBRD study (Holzhacker, and Skakova, 2019), microfinance organizations in Kyrgyzstan occupy a relatively large share of the country's financial market — about 10% of the total outstanding loans — usually financing companies in agriculture, trade and construction. This sector serves a total of 250,000 customers. Despite the fact that most of the loans to microfinance organizations are not secured, the share of overdue debt in this sector was historically low and amounted to no more than 5%. In order to promote the development and sustainability of the microfinance market, the National Bank of the Kyrgyz Republic adopted the National Plan for the Development of the Microfinance Market for 2018–2021 which aims to increase the sector's assets to 5% of GDP by 2021 and cover up to 4.9% of the population with services. It should be noted that starting in 2013, in order to promote the principles of Islamic Finance in this segment of the financial market, the National Bank begins to make changes to the laws on microfinance organizations and credit unions.

At the end of 2018 the National Bank estimated the share of Islamic microfinancing at 4.5% of the total market volume (NBKR, 2019). According to the official register, five out of almost nine hundred micro-credit companies in the country operate on Islamic financial principles: Ak-Karzhi and Companion-Invest in Osh, Ak-Nur Capital, Bereke Finance and M-Bulak in Bishkek. It is noteworthy that *M-Bulak*, being one of the largest micro-financial organizations with an extensive network of offices throughout Kyrgyzstan, provides conventional micro-loans, but Islamic microfinance is issued through a specially created in 2016 Islamic window. The company has its own Shariah Board. Importantly, the development of Islamic microfinance mechanisms began here in 2012. In 2017, M-Bulak signed an Agreement with the IDB and its subsidiary, the Islamic Corporation for Private Sector Development (ICD). It is also known that at the end of 2018, this microfinance company tried to attract Turkapital (Kuwait Finance House), as a shareholder. This comes natural, because according to The Global Competitiveness Report, access to funding is one of the main problems of business in Kyrgyzstan (WEF, 2017). By 2018, the company's portfolio included 13 types of Islamic financial products. However, to date, the Islamic window M-Bulak is focused on 5 of them: qard-hasan (charity loan), istisna (phased financing of construction or production), ijarah and ijarah muntahiyah bittamlik (Islamic leasing), murabaha (resale with a pre-agreed profit margin). All types of Islamic financing are provided by the company in the amount of 5 th to 1 mln som (no more than $12,500) without collateral and guarantees (in some cases, collateral may be required for a loan of $2,500 or more) for a period of 3 months to 7 years[1].

Other Islamic microfinance companies are much smaller. For example, *Ak-Nur Capital*, founded in Bishkek in 2009, belongs to the middle segment of microfinance organizations with an authorized capital of 5 mln som ($72,000). In 2014 the company became a member of the 'Association for the Development of Islamic Economy, Finance and Industry' and was given an opportunity to use the services of the Shariah Board the composition of which had been previously approved by the National Bank. In 2015, Ak-Nur Capital received a special license of the Islamic micro-credit company. Financial results are not published by this company.

Bereke Finance has been operating in Bishkek since 2016, providing microfinance for a period of 1 to 5 years and obtaining equity of investment projects. In addition, the company provides consulting assistance in setting up accounting and marketing for its clients. The company manages its risks by controlling the financial flows of projects and providing guarantees and collateral from funding recipients. The

---

[1] https://mbulak.kg/uploads/2019-04-10-Tablica-nacenok-IPF.pdf

expected return on investment is 15%. However, according to the company's 2019 reports the real return was just slightly over 11%. The portfolio of projects financed by the company is represented by the real sector of the economy: trade, services, construction, etc. In 2019 Bereke Finance attracted 16 mln soms ($200,000) of investments from inviduals, and provided financing for 42 mln soms ($525,000). The company's authorized capital is also 5 mln soms.

Kompanion-Invest was established in Osh as a subsidiary of Kompanion Bank in 2011 and as it is shown by the analysis of audited reports immediately started its activities in accordance with Islamic financial principles[1]. In 2012, the company made its first deal on the murabaha contract. For a period of time, murabaha was its main financial product, but in 2016–2017 the share of this product in the company's portfolio no longer exceeded 50–60% due to the emergence of a new one — ijarah (Islamic leasing). Based on the results of 2017 Kompanion-Invest received 14.5 mln som (more than $200,000) of income from Islamic financial operations. Today, Kompanion-Invest develops its activities through an agents network. Information on *Ak–Karzhy*, a company located in Osh, is not available.

IMF (2016) published the results of a study that showed that 80% of micro, small and medium-sized businesses are interested in obtaining Islamic financing. However, lack of awareness and higher deal structuring costs were identified as problems in the development of the industry. The potential market for Islamic microfinance was estimated at $450 mln.

ISLAMIC LEASING (IJARAH) COMPANIES

Leasing financing in Kyrgyzstan became possible after the adoption of the law 'On Financial Leasing' in 2002. In 2012, preferences were developed and implemented for taxing leasing operations (for example, exemption from sales tax and VAT), which contributed to the emergence of new leasing companies on the market. For example, in 2014, ICD (IDB group), together with Eurasia Group AG, the distributor of the American manufacturer of agricultural machinery John Deere, founded an Islamic leasing (ijarah) company: *Kyrgyzstan Leasing Company* in Bishkek. Later, the founders were joined by Kazakhstan's Islamic leasing company KIC Leasing[2], as well as the investment company Tredstone

---

[1] http://www.k-invest.kg/ru/about/reports
[2] The shareholders of KIC Leasing, as we found out in Chapter 1, are also ICD and Eurasia Group AG.

Capital Partners. Kyrgyzstan Leasing Company started to carry out operations in 2015. According to the official website, it finances the purchase of machinery and equipment by businesses in the amount of $15 to 500 th for up to 5 years and with the initiator's own funds in the amount of 20% of the cost of equipment. The company's financial statements are not made public, but we were able to find a number of its deals: the launch of a taxi service with its own cars fleet, the purchase of vehicles for a cargo carrier company and equipment for a confectionery house. Still, it seems that most of the deals are financed by this ijarah company with the aim of purchasing John Deere agricultural equipment by local farmers. Otherwise, the business logic of entering the capital of Kyrgyzstan Leasing Company by the distributor of American equipment cannot be explained. This feature is in the trend of the leasing market of Kyrgyzstan, where the main property leased is agricultural machinery (USAID, 2016).

Thus, 1 out of 11 leasing companies operates according to Islamic financial principles. It is worth noting that among all the Islamic financing instruments, ijarah is perhaps the least different from conventional leasing. However, even in this case, an Islamic financial company carries greater risks compared to conventional institutions. In general, leasing makes a great contribution against poverty and inequality allowing entrepreneurs who have only a small part of the funds necessary to purchase transport or equipment to start their own businesses.

ISLAMIC INSURANCE (TAKAFUL) AND ISSUE OF ISLAMIC BONDS (SUKUK)

In 2014, the government of Kyrgyzstan, the IDB and Simmons & Simmons, an international law firm, signed an Agreement on the development of draft laws on the introduction of Islamic insurance (takaful) and Islamic securities (sukuk). Simmons & Simmons services were funded under the IDB technical assistance grant. Based on the available data, in 2014, an attempt was made to establish an Islamic insurance company based on EcoIslamicBank[1], but apparently it was unsuccessful. In 2015 the Kyrgyz Parliament approved the draft amendments on Islamic mortgage-backed securities, and in 2016 these amendments were made to the law 'On the Securities Market'. Their goal was to introduce new financial instruments: Islamic lease certificates (sukuk al-ijarah); Islamic project finance certificates (sukuk

---

[1] http://www.asn-news.ru/smi/13951

70

al-istisna); Islamic equity certificates (sukuk al-mudaraba); Islamic investment agency certificates (sukuk al-wakala bi al-istithmar); and Islamic partnership certificates (sukuk al-musharaka). The adopted law introduced a new Chapter on the specifics of the issue and circulation of Islamic securities, clarified the requirements for the issue, supplemented the rules on the repayment of Islamic securities, and defined the organizational and legal form of the Islamic special financial company (SPV).

In July 2017, during the annual Bishkek International Financial Forum, Chairman of the National Bank of Kyrgyzstan T. Abdygulov noted: "The development of Islamic principles of financing in Kyrgyzstan will enable the population to use alternative types of financing which will strengthen the competitive environment in the banking and financial sector of the country and, as a result, improve the quality of banking and financial products"[1]. Thus, the above allows us to conclude that the National Bank adheres to the policy of stimulating financial innovation and encouraging a variety of market instruments.

At the end of 2019 the State Mortgage Company presented a new program for 2020–2025. This program was the first to introduce Islamic securities and housing certificates as new financial instruments for increasing the volume of residential construction and attracting additional investment in the volume of up to 1.25 bln som[2] ($15.6 mln).

Thus, the Islamic financial market of Kyrgyzstan is represented by two Islamic banks, five microfinance and one Islamic leasing companies. The Islamic Development Bank has invested more than $0.3 bln in a wide range of projects, from education to energy. The total volume of Islamic investments in Kyrgyzstan aimed at implementing about 80 identified deals is estimated at more than $0.8 bln.

Local authorities are quite consistent in creating a regulatory framework and general institutional environment for the development of this financial sector. However, while noting the weakness of institutions and significant political instability in the country, OSCE professor A. Wolters (2013) stressed that "Islamic finance seems not to rely solely on state support for its development <...> initiatives mostly come from actors from non-government sectors". He notes that "after the financial crisis, however, the double effect of a real-economy need for new and fresh cash-flows and the rising discourse of and the search for alternative

---

[1] https://knews.kg/2017/06/02/razvitie-islamskih-printsipov-finansirovaniya-v-kr-povysit-kachestvo-bankovskih-i-finansovyh-produktov-nb-kr/

[2] https://ru.sputnik.kg/society/20191220/1046564180/kyrgyzstan-gosudarstvennaya-ipotechnaya-programma-kredity-proekt.html

forms of banking has opened a new chapter for Islamic Finance in the region of Central Asia". According to D. Hoggarth (2016), "the most democratic of the post-Soviet central Asian republics, Kyrgyzstan has viewed Islamic Finance favorably, realizing the economic benefits of market diversification". Moreover, according to D. Hoggarth (2016), "Islamic finance have the potential to alter the surrounding geopolitical relationships". Thus, our research has shown that despite the yet modest market volumes, Islamic Finance has further growth prospects which are associated with the arrival of large foreign Islamic banks and the issuance of Islamic securities.

In general, since gaining independence, Kyrgyzstan has been more open and consistent in the development of Islamic Finance compared to other Central Asian and Transcaucasian countries. There is an understanding of the need for the initial development of the market by its own forces, which will prepare it for the arrival of larger foreign Islamic capital, e.g., through implementation of M&A-deals or creation of joint ventures.

CHAPTER 6.
TAJIKISTAN

According to its socio-economic indicators, Tajikistan is the poorest country in the post-Soviet region. The economy of this country is formed by mining, metal processing, agriculture and remittances from citizens working abroad, mainly in Russia and Kazakhstan[1]. The country is rich in minerals, and exports aluminum, gold, zinc, lead and copper (Appendix A). Tajikistan's industry mainly consists of small but outdated food and textile factories, large hydroelectric power plants, and the Talco aluminum plant, which, however, is not operating at full capacity.

The high level of Tajikistan's debt, currently amounting to more than 35% of GDP ($2.9 bln)[2], can be a source of financial instability. This is aggravated by the fact that the country's largest lender is the Chinese Eximbank (the Export-Import Bank of China), which accounts for more than 40% of the total external debt. In addition, Tajikistan has major debt commitments to the International Development Association of the World Bank group (11%), the Asian Development Bank (9%), as well as the Islamic Development Bank (5%) and members of the Arab Coordination Group (5%)[3], as shown in Fig. 6.1. China has been the country's largest lender and investor for many years[4]. However, both the Islamic Development Bank and Arab investors have invested considerable funds in the economy of Tajikistan in recent years, which have been used to implement projects that are significant for the economy and society. Next we will discuss the role of Islamic capital and Islamic Finance in the economy of Tajikistan in detail. To do this, we have collected and analyzed the content of an empirical database consisting of about 70 deals involving capital invested in Tajikistan in accordance with Islamic financial principles.

---

[1] According to various estimates, the total number of Tajik citizens working abroad is more than 1 mln (with a total population of more than 9 mln), and their remittances to families account for more than 30% of Tajikistan's GDP.

[2] https://tajikta.tj/ru/news/s-nachala-goda-vneshniy-dolg-tadzhikistana-sokratilsya-na-10-mln-i-sostavil-2-mlrd-890-1-mln

[3] In March 2020 Tajikistan's debt to the Saudi Fund for Development was $78,1 mln, the OPEC Fund for International Development — $40.4 mln, the Kuwait Fund for Arab Economic Development — $37.4 mln, the Abu Dhabi Fund for Development — $9.7 mln.

[4] According to the Ministry of Finance of Tajikistan, at the end of 2018 the share of private foreign investment of China was 51%, followed by the United Kingdom (10%).

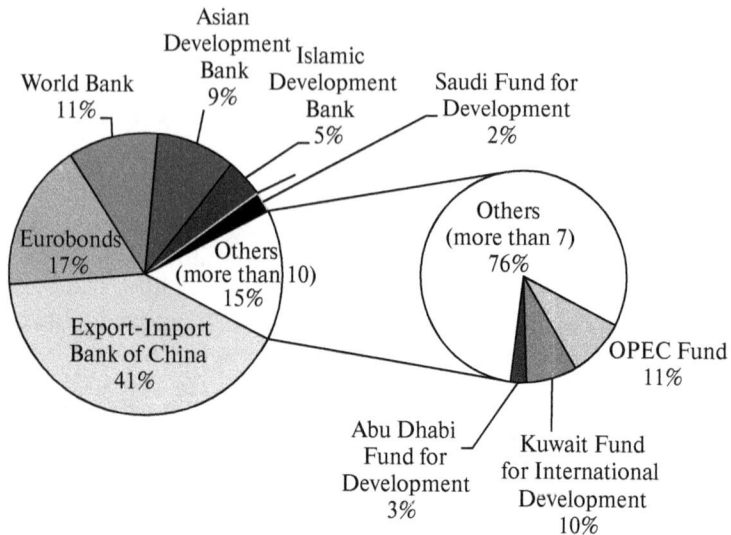

Fig. 6.1. Structure of Tajikistan's public debt at the end of 2018.
Source: based on the data of the Ministry of Finance of the Republic
of Tajikistan (MoF, 2018)

ISLAMIC DEVELOPMENT BANK GROUP

In 1996 Tajikistan, being a member of the Organization of the Islamic Conference, became a member of the Islamic Development Bank (IDB). Since then, the country has attracted almost $0.5 bln in investment from this development bank to implement more than 60 projects. We estimate the average size of the IDB deal in Tajikistan at more than $7 mln. The country's share in the IDB's subscribed capital of is 0.04%, and the amount paid for this share (Paid-Up Capital) was $18.2 mln (Appendix B).

Half of the funds raised from the IDB was invested in 3 sectors — road construction, education and irrigation, and another third — in energy sector, agriculture and healthcare, as shown in Table 6.1. Almost a tenth of the IDB's investment in the country accounts for the financial sector, which includes microfinance, development of Islamic financial infrastructure, and support for small and medium-sized businesses through Tajik banks. In addition, the IDB's investments were directed to the real estate sector, public administration, as well as emergency assistance to victims of flooding and adverse weather conditions.

Table 6.1. The IDB deals in Tajikistan

Sector	Number of IDB deals, pcs.	Total investment by the IDB, $ mln	Share in total investment, %
Road construction	8	91.5	18.7
Education	9	77.7	16.0
Water supply and irrigation	6	77.4	15.8
Energy	5	59	12.0
Agriculture	6	55.7	11.5
Healthcare	6	54.3	11.0
Finance	13	40.8	8.3
Real Estate	3	30.2	6.2
Public administration	6	1.3	0.3
Emergency assistance	2	0.4	0.1
Total	64	488.3	99.9

Source: calculation based on Appendix C.

The largest investment projects of the IDB in the Republic of Tajikistan were the CASA-1000 ($70 mln), the irrigation system in Dangara district (more than $50 mln), the construction of schools ($47 mln), the Shogun–Zigar road (more than $41 mln) and the Kulyab–Kalaikhumb road ($40 mln). These 5 projects together account for half of the total investment of this development bank.

We will start a brief overview of the IDB's deals with analysis of the *road construction sector*, the expansion of which is an important factor in the economic growth of any country. It should be noted that 90% of the territory of Tajikistan is mountainous, which significantly complicates any road construction project and increases their cost. Two major projects account for almost 90% of the total value of the IDB's deals in this sector. The first of them is the construction of the *Shogun–Zigar highway* along the Panj river, which runs along the border with Afghanistan. The road was designed not only to improve the country's territorial integrity, but also to connect Tajikistan with the strategic Karakoram highway in China and the deep-water port of Karachi in Pakistan. The project included the construction of 40 km of the road and bridges and was estimated at more than $90 mln. Besides financing all the 3 stages of the project from 2001 to 2019 for more than $40 mln, the IDB also attracted co-investors — members of the Arab Coordination Group. The government of Tajikistan co-financed the implementation of the project in the amount of $7 mln.

The IDB also invested a similar amount ($40.2 mln) in another road project — the reconstruction of the 58-km *Kulyab–Kalaikhumb highway*. Along with widening and leveling the road, the construction work included installing water pipes, stabilizing mountain slopes, building protective foundations, bridges, and a tunnel. The IDB also attracted members of the Arab Coordination Group: for example, the OPEC Fund for International Development invested $27 mln, and the Kuwait Fund for Arab Economic Development — $7.5 mln[1]. The Asian Development Bank also was an investor of that large and multi-stage project. It invested $20 mln.

The education sector, which has faced significant difficulties due to physical damage (caused by civil unrest) and reduced funding (as a result of the general economic downturn in the 1990s), ranks second in the structure of the IDB's investment in Tajikistan. As you can see in Table 6.1, the IDB has invested about $78 mln in this sphere for a long term (on average for 25 years). a small amount of funds was allocated for the construction of religious educational institutions ($259,000), the main part of the capital was invested in the *construction and equipment of secondary schools*, which was implemented in 3 stages from 1998 to 2017. Schools were built in 13 districts of the country and designed to train more than 12,000 children and employ more than 1,300 teachers. The project was co-financed by the government of Tajikistan, and its ultimate goal was enhancing literacy and reducing poverty among rural population. In 2013 a $10 mln tranche from the IDB was allocated for the construction of schools in rural areas, for conducting vocational education, training and providing students with microfinance.

The IDB also invested heavily in the construction of the country's *irrigation system*, which is rich in natural water resources. The project that received the most funding was the *Dungarin valley irrigation system*. In 1997 the IDB funded the feasibility study of the project. The first stage of the project implementation started in 2001, and the third stage continues to this day. The co-investors of the IDB, which invested more than $50 mln, were the aforementioned Kuwait Fund for Arab Economic Development ($4 mln) and the government of Tajikistan. The project should provide irrigation of 1,750 hectares of new land, which will increase the crops of cotton, wheat, vegetables and forage crops. In addition, more than 13,000 new jobs should be created there. a similar project was launched in 2019 in *Khatlon region*. Its value is $53.5 mln,

---

[1] See i) https://opecfund.org/operations ii) https://www.kuwait-fund.org/en/web/kfund/table

the investors are the IDB — $15 mln and members of the Arab Coordination Group (the Saudi Fund for Development — $25 mln and the OPEC Fund for International Development — $10 mln), the share of the government of Tajikistan is $3.5 mln. The project aims to improve the living standards of 60,000 rural residents and create 2,000 permanent and 15,000 seasonal jobs. In general, water supply projects are of great importance for the economy, as they can significantly increase irrigation areas and improve food security.

In the country's *energy sector*, the IDB finances hydroelectric projects which are of great importance to the economy. For example, this was the *construction of small hydroelectric power plants* in 8 rural areas experiencing energy shortages, where the bank had invested $12mln. The facilities were completed in 2015. Despite a number of other projects, let's take a closer look at one of them — *CASA-1000[1]* which was planned in the early 2000s and was more political in nature. The project, with a total cost of more than $1 bln, is designed to transfer 1,000 MW of electricity to Pakistan and 300 MW to Afghanistan, which requires the construction of high-voltage transmission lines from Kyrgyzstan and Tajikistan with a length of more than 1,200 km. The share of electricity exports from Tajikistan within the framework of CASA-1000 will be 70%, and from Kyrgyzstan — 30%. The World Bank's contribution to the project is equal to half of its cost ($526.5 mln). The cost of the Tajik part of the project is $314 mln, the Afghan part — $354 mln, the Kyrgyz and Pakistani parts — $209 mln each. According to the media, the IDB has allocated $70 mln to Tajikistan. In addition, the Tajik government has received loans from the European Bank for Reconstruction and Development ($110 mln), the World Bank ($45 mln), the European Investment Bank ($70 mln), and the governments of Great Britain and Australia. The share of the government of Tajikistan in this project is $15 mln. The official launch of the CASA-1000 was in 2016, and it is planned to be completed in 2020–2021. The project is implemented by such large international companies as ABB from Sweden, Kalpataru Power Transmission from India, CESI from Italy, and Monenko Iran Consulting Engineers from Iran. As an argument for the implementation of CASA-1000, the government of Tajikistan cited, on the one hand, the presence of significant and growing demand for electricity in South Asia, and, on the other, the annual idle discharge of water in the summer period in Tajikistan, which is equivalent to the production of 5 bln cubic

---

[1] This project is international and has already been mentioned in the previous Chapter.

meters kW/h of electricity, which according to their estimates is more than $200 mln.

The bank's investments in the *healthcare sector* amounted to more than $50 mln. Thus, in 2014 $400,000 of them were provided for the prevention of *mother-to-child transmission of HIV/AIDS*. At the time of the project implementation, the number of people with this infection in the country was estimated at 6,000, one third of them were women, including 500 pregnant women. The reason for the problem is the lack of proper medical examination of migrant workers upon their return from Russia[1]. Another project in this sector is *'improving the quality of medical care services for mothers and children in 4 districts of Khatlon region'*. In 2019 its amount was almost $27 mln, of which $23 mln was the funds of the IDB, one-third of that was provided in the form of a grant and two-thirds — in the form of returnable financing according to Islamic principles for a period of 20 years. The share of the government of Tajikistan in the project is about $4 mln. Its implementation period is 2019—2025.

The financial sector as an investment object of the IDB includes 3 areas in our study: funding of an Islamic leasing company ($21 mln), Islamic microfinance of business through local banks ($11mln), and technical assistance to the institutional development of Islamic Finance in the country ($0.5 mln). We will discuss them in detail below.

Having analyzed the IDB's deals, we found out the following features of the investment strategy of this development institution in Tajikistan:

- *firstly,* the IDB's investment interests in Tajikistan are quite extensive, ranging from educational to energy projects;
- *secondly,* the distribution of the IDB's capital across sectors and projects is diversified;
- *thirdly,* the IDB co-finances projects together with other multilateral development banks, such as the World Bank, the Asian Development Bank, the European Bank for Reconstruction and Development, and members of the Arab Coordination Group. In addition, the government of Tajikistan acts as a co-investor in almost all major deals (but in a smaller proportion), which is probably a critical condition for obtaining financing from the IDB.

---

[1] There are more than 1 mln people with HIV living in Russia. The country ranks 11th in the world after ten African countries. The HIV prevalence in Russia is 1.2, which is 6 times as high as in Tajikistan (0.2).

ISLAMIC BANKS

The introduction of Islamic banking in Tajikistan was first discussed during the global financial crisis of 2008—2009. It was then that the appeal of the government of the country on the introduction of Islamic banking to the National Bank of Tajikistan appeared. In 2010, together with *Sohibkorbank*[1] it conducted a study of the market's need for Islamic banking that proved to be high enough[2]. In 2011 the issue of Islamic banking began to be considered at a specially created interdepartmental commission. Concurrently, extensive educational work was being carried out among financial market participants in the form of presentations and trainings in the central banks of the countries participating in the Organization of the Islamic Conference.

In 2012 with the support of the IDB, as well as consultations in Kyrgyzstan, where the first Islamic bank started its official work in 2007, Sohibkorbank developed a draft law on Islamic banking. a little later, the IDB provided technical assistance to the National Bank of Tajikistan in the amount of more than $150,000. It was aimed at paying for the services of legal consultants — Zaid Ibrahim & Co[3], an international company of Malaysian origin — to develop amendments to the Tajik legislation. The amendments were made, and the law 'On Islamic banking' was adopted by the local government in the summer of 2014. With the adoption of the law, the National Bank, on the one hand, expected to attract foreign Islamic investors to the banking sector, on the other — to restore public confidence in the country's banking system in the post-crisis period.

When speaking about the public's confidence in the banking sector in Tajikistan, we should focus on the problems of the sector:

- *firstly,* it is a high level of concentration (4 large banks account for 75% of total assets and 80% of all deposits);
- *secondly,* it is a liquidity crisis that some systemically important banks periodically face, which makes them dependent on government support;
- *thirdly,* it is a weak diversification of the loan portfolio, especially in systemically important banks (ADB, 2016b).

The reasons for these problems, which periodically lead to banking crises, are: related and special-purpose lending, administrative

---

[1] It was founded in 1999; since then, it has changed owners several times; it is one of the ten largest banks in the country. Its staff is more than 300 employees.

[2] http://www.dialog.tj/news/razvitie-alternativnykh-finansovykh-instrumentov-mozhet-sokratit-rasstoyanie-mezhdu-dengami-i-biznesom

[3] Now referred to as ZICO Law.

interference, weak risk management, poor quality of corporate governance and banks' accountability to their minority shareholders. When these and other problems caused a drop in public confidence in the country's banking system in 2008–2009, the authorities began to look for salvation in the Islamic banking model. For example, Agroinvestbank and Tajikistan Development Bank (part of the Tojiksodirotbank group), which at that time were experiencing problems with liquidity, announced the attraction of Islamic capital and the transition to Islamic financial principles, but they failed to achieve great success in negotiations with Islamic investors. It is only known that in 2009 the IDB allocated a little more than $1.5 mln to Tojiksodirotbank and $2.5 mln to Amonatbank to develop microfinancing in rural areas.

The head of the National Bank did not veil the goals of further development of legislation in the field of Islamic banking and stated: "<...> Today the economy of Tajikistan is in great need of investment. It is expected that Islamic banking will help expand the range of banking operations, find new sources of external financing, as well as of internal deposits"[1]. Indeed, Qatari investors began to show interest in the development of the Islamic banking industry: for example, the Chairman of Ezdan Holding, Sheikh Dr. Khalid bin Thani bin Abdullah Al Thani, during his meeting with E. Rahmon noted, "the creation of the first Islamic bank could be another initiative in the framework of bilateral relations between Qatar and Tajikistan"[2]. However, due to the financial crisis that began in the country in 2015 and was associated with a reduction in remittances, and a number of other risks, the project was frozen. It was then that the country's banking system once again faced difficulties[3].

The interest of Qatari investors, and not any other investors, in Tajikistan is not accidental: since 2012 Qatari Diar, owned by the Qatar Investment Authority, has been building the *Diar Dushanbe[4] complex* there. In 2017 progress in implementing Islamic principles in the economy was discussed by officials — D. Nurmakhmadzoda,

---

[1] https://tajikta.tj/ru/news/banki-tadzhikistana-zainteresovany-rabotat-po-printsipam-islamskogo-bankinga-nbt

[2] https://rus.ozodi.org/a/26599500.html

[3] Two banks — Tajik Prombank and Fononbank — went bankrupt, and the government of Tajikistan issued bills of credit for the amount of about $490 mln in favor of the other two — Tajiksodirotbank and Agroinvestbank.

[4] This is a luxurious development project that consists of residential buildings, office buildings, a boutique hotel, shopping and entertainment spaces. The Qatari side estimated its investment in this project at $300 mln.

the Chairman of the National Bank of Tajikistan, and Abdulla bin Saoud Al-Thani, the Governor of Qatar Central Bank. However, Qatari investors did not open an Islamic bank here, and the only bank operating on Islamic financial principles to date was founded in 2019 by converting and renaming the aforementioned Sohibkorbank to the *Tawhidbank*. The bank's transformation from conventional to Islamic took place during a year with the support of the Islamic Corporation for the Development of the Private Sector (ICD) from the IDB group. One of the main elements of the transformation was the introduction of a special automated system, the supplier of which was the International Turnkey Systems from Kuwait. In addition, the bank has established its own Shariah Board headed by Dr. Muhammad Akram Laldin, the rector of the Malaysian International Shariah Research Academy for Islamic Finance, a member of 16 Shariah boards around the world, including the committee of the Kyrgyz EcoIslamicBank. The products offered by the bank include financing in the form of murabaha and deposits in the form of limited and unlimited mudaraba. It is not possible to analyze the results of the bank's financial activities and the scale of its operations, as the audited financial statements for 2019 have not been published yet.

When entrusting a special license to an Islamic bank for the first time, D. Nurmakhmadzoda, the Chairman of the National Bank of Tajikistan, said, this "event has become a new page in the banking history of the country <...> issuing a license to an Islamic bank will help attract foreign investment and establish other Islamic banks"[1]. However, to date, only 1 out of 17 banks in the country is Islamic. The *Alif Samroya*, a micro-credit company which was founded in 2014 and positioned itself as an Islamic one, apparently is not. This company works with elements of Islamic financial principles: for example, it does not set a fixed interest rate on deposits, but calculates it depending on the return on assets; it does not provide funding for sinful (haram) activities related to alcohol, gambling, and others. However, the analysis of the financial statements shows that the company receives interest income and issues loans to customers[2]. The Islamic financial principles claimed by the company are more of a marketing ploy. However, we do not rule out the full transition of the Alif Samroy to the Islamic bank, which, as the experience of the Tawhidbank shows, is only a matter of time and support from the specialized structures of the IDB.

---

[1] https://tj.sputniknews.ru/country/20190917/1029878040/nacbank-tajikistan-licenziya-islamskiy-bank.html
[2] https://alif.tj/files/BS_and_P&L_audited.pdf

ISLAMIC LEASING (IJARAH) COMPANIES

In early 2013 the ICD from the IDB group, together with a co-investor, established the Islamic *ASR Leasing LLC* in Tajikistan with an authorized capital of $3 mln. Currently, the only co-investor of ICD is the Swiss Eurasia Group AG, which owns similar assets in other CIS countries. Analyzing the financial operations of the IDB, we noted that in 2017 it capitalized ASR Leasing LLC in the amount of $20 mln[1]. We failed to find information about the deals of this leasing company, and it also does not publish financial statements, so it is impossible to conduct any objective analysis of its activities. However, according to the information on the official website, ASR Leasing LLC provides Islamic leasing financing to small and medium-sized businesses for a period of 1–4 years with an advance payment of at least 20% of the project cost. In general, despite the reforms carried out by the government of Tajikistan in order to eliminate double taxation and customs duties, the leasing industry remains small, and its growth is constrained by the lack of access to long-term capital (ADB, 2016).

Thus, our analysis has shown that Islamic Finance is gradually forming a new, albeit not so significant segment in the economy of Tajikistan. We estimate the total volume of Islamic capital involved in the implementation of about 70 deals as more than $0.5 bln, but it is mainly formed by investments of the Islamic Development Bank. However, there is also a private initiative there, and the examples of the micro-credit company Alif Samroya and the first Islamic bank Tawhidbank prove that.

A. Wolters (2013) notes that "irrespective of such favorable indications, Islamic financing has been very poorly developed in Tajikistan". However, Islamic Finance should be considered in a complex and should not be taken out of the context of the overall level of development of the country's financial system. For example, in Tajikistan, capital markets are also poorly developed: corporate bonds are not actually issued there, and only small issues of short-term sovereign bonds are made from time to time, and the National Bank occasionally issues deposit certificates, for which no secondary market has actually been created (ADB, 2016b). In 2011 they adopted law on the capital market which covers all its aspects: underwriting, brokerage operations, deals, asset management, depository and regulator, but since then no additional regulations have been issued. In general, Tajikistan's

---

[1] https://www.isdb.org/projects/data

financial system is characterized by high concentration, a low level of competition and mediation, and absolute dominance of the banking sector. We believe that the weak level of development of the country's financial system is the first factor limiting the development of Islamic Finance there. Besides, A. Wolters (2013) highlights such an important factor as the decline in the level of freedoms that he has observed there since 2011. He cites examples: the ban of the only Islamic Renaissance Party in the Central Asian region, new restrictions on religious practices, and violations in parliamentary elections. "There is reason to believe that this caution is rooted in political considerations <...> Tajikistan's struggle against alleged Islamist groups, the competition of Rahmon's regime with the Islamic Renaissance Party and the attempt to attract the big powers' attention feed a discourse that warns of an imminent Islamist threat," he writes in his work. This factor also limits the investment of large foreign Islamic investors. Nevertheless, the development of Islamic banking and stock financing instruments is stated to be the goal of the national development strategy of Tajikistan until 2030. And, despite the limitations and difficulties, Islamic financial companies have almost limitless opportunities: for example, only 11.5% of the local adult population have an account with at least one financial institution, 4.8% have a bank loan, 0.3% — official savings and 0.8% — voluntary health insurance (ADB, 2016b).

CHAPTER 7.
RUSSIA

In the entire European space, Russia is home to the largest number of Muslims. According to various estimates, the number of the Muslim population in Russia is up to 25 mln people[1]. According to Pew Research (2015) forecasts until 2050 Russia will continue to be the country with the largest Muslim population in Europe. As for the CIS countries, more Muslims live only in Uzbekistan (more than 30 mln people). Russian Muslims are part of more than 40 ethnic groups and historically inhabit the Volga region, Western Siberia, and the North Caucasus. However, in other parts of the Russian Federation, such as Moscow and Saint Petersburg, adherents of Islam also make up a significant part of the local population. Today, the ethnic Muslim population is concentrated in seven regions of the Russian Federation: Tatarstan and Bashkortostan in the Volga region and Chechnya, Ingushetia, Dagestan, Kabardino-Balkaria and Karachay-Cherkessia in the North Caucasus. The largest Muslim nation in Russia is the Tatars, who number up to 6 mln people (4% of the population). They are followed by Bashkirs (up to 1.5 mln people, or 1.1%), Chechens (1.4 mln people, or 1%) and others.

After the collapse of the Soviet Union and the collapse of the Communist ideology, Russian Muslims began to rediscover conventional Islamic values. This inevitably led to intellectual pursuit and discussions about life according to Shariah. The topic of Islamic Finance was not an exception, moreover, it became a significant part of the discourse on fair structure of the country's economic system. Besides, the interest in the phenomenon of Islamic Finance was reinforced by the incredible success of this project in the Middle East, South-East Asia and Western Europe, as well as their resistance to crisis phenomena (Hasan, and Dridi, 2010). Therefore, it is logical that with the further strengthening of the religious identity of Russian Muslims, the topic of Islamic Finance will be raised again and again in the public discussion.

In Russia, interest in this topic resulted in more modest practices as compared to Malaysia or the Gulf countries but still quite diverse. Here, the history of Islamic Finance can be traced since the collapse

---

[1] Thus, according to the Central Intelligence Agency, the share of Russian Muslims is 10–15% of the total population, and according to Pew Research (2015), it was 10% of the population in 2010 and is expected to reach 16.8% in 2050.

of the USSR: *the first Islamic bank Badr-Forte* was founded in Moscow in 1991 (however, the Bank's license was revoked in 2006). In 1992, an attempt was made to create an Islamic bank in Kemerovo. For exactly one year, from 2004 to 2005, a special Department of Islamic Insurance operates within the framework of the *Tatarstan insurance company Itil* (now referred to as Armeec). At the same time, many regional banks start issuing Islamic debit cards. BrokerCreditService launches *Halal, a mutual investment fund* developed according to the Dow Jones Islamic Shariah methodology. *Linova,* a new company created in Kazan starts providing services for attracting corporate finance based on principles of Islamic Finance. In 2008, an investment conference with the support of the Islamic Development Bank is also held in Kazan. Later, this conference develops into the annual international economic summit *'Russia - the Islamic World: KazanSummit'* (Nagimova, 2018b). In 2009, the topic of Islamic Finance was developed by the Council of Muftis of Russia which opened a special department for this purpose. At the same time, VTB Capital, having launched an office in the UAE, declares its intention to promote the market of Islamic bonds (sukuk). In 2010, the government of the Republic of Tatarstan, the Islamic Development Bank, and investors from Kuwait, Yemen, and Saudi Arabia established the *Tatarstan International Investment Company* to provide Islamic financing in the Russian market. In the same year, *Yumart Finance* was founded in Kazan, and began to provide Islamic financing to businesses and the public. In 2011, *Financial House Amal* is launched in Kazan where it works with businesses and wealthy clients according to Islamic standards. Later Yumart Finance and Amal merge, and now the company operates under the brand 'Financial House 'Amal'. In the same year, the Islamic financial company *LaRiba* starts working in Dagestan on the basis of Expressbank. In 2013, the bank's license is revoked, but the Islamic financial company remains afloat and exists to this day. In 2012, the Euro-Polis insurance company (now Absolute Insurance) insures the *Kazan Al-Marjani mosque* in accordance with the takaful Shariah standard and starts providing Islamic financial products in Moscow, Saint Petersburg, Kazan, Ufa and Nizhny Novgorod. In 2013, *Ellipse Bank* of Nizhny Novgorod opens its third Islamic window in Saratov (previously, Islamic windows were opened by the Bank in Nizhny Novgorod and Ufa), but in 2014 this Bank also loses its license. In 2014, The Association of Russian Banks sends an open letter to the Central Bank justifying the introduction of legislative amendments for the full operation of Islamic banks. In 2014, the *International Bank of*

Azerbaijan[1] enters the Russian market of Islamic banking services. In the same year, the *Russian National Rating Agency* signed an Agreement with the Islamic International Rating Agency (Bahrain) on joint rating of Islamic financial products in Russia. In 2011 and 2015, the Tatarstan *Ak Bars Bank* attracted a total of $160mln of investments from Islamic capital markets (Nagimova, 2018b). During 2015, at the height of anti-Russian political sanctions imposed by Western countries, a number of draft laws on Islamic Finance were submitted to the State Duma, but they were rejected in the same year. The media reports about the negotiations of the Bahraini Islamic banks *Al Baraka* and *Al Shamal* with local players. At the same time, the management of *Sberbank* declares its intention to develop Islamic banking services in regions with a dominant Muslim population Tatarstan being selected as a pilot region. In the autumn of 2015, a working group on Islamic Finance is created at the Central Bank, and launches a feasibility study for opening Islamic windows in Tatarstan. The study is supported by a grant from the Malaysian government. In 2016, *Center of Partner Banking* is established in Kazan with the support of the local TatAgroPromBank, which, however, was closed after a year of operation due to the revocation of the Bank's license. In 2016 and 2017, an *annual Gaidar Forum* is held to host public discussions on the topic of Islamic Finance. At the end of 2016, the *International Association of Islamic Business* was founded, whose goal, among others, is to "promote the creation of a modern credit and financial system based on the principles of fairness and mutually beneficial partnership participation". a technical issue of Islamic bonds (sukuk) in 2017 simultaneously meets both the current Russian legislation and the Shariah standards. In recent years, Sberbank has provided support for holding round tables on Islamic Finance. In addition, Sberbank organizes one-off closed corporate finance deals based on the Islamic financial principles. Despite all the above mentioned, Sberbank is still not represented in the retail market, e.g., in the format of Islamic windows.

Today, the market of Islamic Finance in Russia is actually represented by sporadic deals of corporate Islamic Finance (information on which gets little media coverage); a number of microfinance companies providing financing on Islamic principles to the population and small and medium-sized businesses in Tatarstan, Dagestan and Chechnya; and companies that provide goods or services in installments (housing savings cooperative Housing traditions, trading firm Kirgu, etc.). Indirectly,

---

[1] See Chapter 3.

the market of Islamic Finance can also include deals financed through joint platforms of the Russian Direct Investment Fund[1] and sovereign funds of the Gulf which are similar in their economic essence to Islamic Finance, though, in the absence of a special law on Islamic Finance in Russia, can ultimately be regarded as such (Nagimova, 2018b).

As for previous research on this topic, the above mentioned scholar D.Hoggarth (2016) has studied Islamic Finance in the context of post-colonial market-building in Central Asia and Russia. In her work, she points out that in contrast to the Central Asian countries, Islamic Finance is a "less obvious choice" for Russia. Previously, "the Russian state has been challenged by the role of Islam in the Caucasus, but it has gone to considerable lengths to retain ties with Islamic countries that offer synergies with Russia's political and economic agenda", which is especially relevant in the context of anti-Russian sanctions imposed by Western countries. In her opinion, the current interest of the Russian state in the topic of Islamic Finance is caused by the reinforcement of "the Russian colonial identity in the Caucasus and Central Asia through the ideational projection of religious tolerance". Turning to the works of Russian scholars we should note the contribution of R. Bekkin (2007) to the theoretical understanding of the Islamic economy and the parallels he drew with the socialist and capitalist doctrines. From the angle of our research, we should highlight the work "Islamic Finance: Opportunities for the Russian Economy" by B. Chokaev (2015), who comes to the conclusion that Russia needs to create "an infrastructure that allows the subjects of this industry to function on equal terms with other subjects of the financial system in terms of financial, tax and administrative aspects". B. Chokaev sees a possible solution to this problem in "the creation of a new (or improvement of the existing) organizational and legal form" of Islamic financial companies. Our research significantly expands and deepens these conclusions using a sociological approach.

In the spring of 2020, we conducted a research using the *qualitative method of in-depth expert interviews*. The duration of each interview organized according to a specially developed guide ranged from 30 to 60 minutes. The respondent group included 10 experts on Islamic Finance representing banks, funds, Islamic Finance and consulting companies. The respondents were persons occupying senior positions:

---

[1] It was established on the initiative of the President and Prime Minister of the Russian Federation in 2011. The fund makes direct investments in projects of Russian companies through joint platforms created with the largest sovereign wealth funds of all the Gulf countries except Oman. In 2016, this fund left the VneshEconomBank group and also received the status of a sovereign wealth fund.

shareholders, General and Managing Directors, as well as heads of departments.

The respondents were asked to describe their understanding of the growth limits of the Islamic Finance market, the degree of competitiveness of Islamic Finance, and their target audience in Russia. The position of experts on this range of issues is all the more important because the Central Bank hardly recognizes the existence of the Islamic Finance market. In addition, the research was focused not only on the history and practices, but also on the respondents' personal ideas about the future of Islamic Finance and the model of its further implementation in the Russian economy.

To analyze the interview texts, we additionally used another qualitative method: the *method of cognitive mapping* which was developed and actively used by a team of scholars lead by R. Axelrod (1976), an American political scientist. This method allows to create cognitive maps by identifying persistent connectives repeated in the speech of respondents. The essence of the method is to graphically display the concepts (concepts and relationships between them) that are most often used by respondents. To build the final map (Appendix D), we selected connectives (the concept of 'cause' — connective — the concept of 'effect') that were found in the speech of at least six of the ten interviewees (for most of the connectives, this indicator was higher) provided that no other respondents expressed a direct denial of this connective. The concepts were formulated in such a way as to most accurately reflect the general meaning of the statements of various experts.

IS ISLAMIC FINANCE COMPETITIVE IN RUSSIA?

In this set of questions, together with the experts, we discussed the cost of Islamic capital: if it is more expensive than interest-based capital, and the main practical advantages of Islamic Finance for business and the population.

Speaking about global capital markets, one of the respondents said: "There is a global market and the flow of capital in it, due to which the value of money is leveled". Moreover, Islamic investors are "willing to sacrifice certain returns for the sake of stability". As for the local market, according to another expert, "the fact that it [Islamic Finance][1] can be more expensive in Russia is only due to the lack of a properly functioning infrastructure, so companies providing services based on Islamic financial

---

[1] Here and further, the author's notes are shown in square brackets.

principles have higher maintenance costs. This is a consequence of this sector being underdeveloped in Russia". All the experts unanimously noted that the services of Islamic financial companies are competitive in cost, and the head of one of these companies explained: "Our services might be more expensive in some cases, but in general we are 'in the market'. We compared car loan conditions. Conventional banks are tricky in this regard: offering a low interest rate, they actually make profit by selling additional services: insurance services, commissions. However, buying a car on credit involves the cost of GOLD insurance policy: failing to purchase it will make the interest rate higher".

One of our experts noted that in general, "there is always a demand for financial products, otherwise there would not be such a large number of banks, microfinance and micro-credit companies on the market. <...> The population and business definitely need it". The same expert gave a very succinct description of Islamic Finance as "financial products that carry additional characteristics: no fines, penalties, and a fixed amount under the agreement". Another respondent drew attention to the fact that Islamic Finance "is very similar to the instruments of ethical finance in Europe, which are very close to Shariah standards".

According to the respondents' responses, there are at least four competitive advantages for Islamic Finance. First of all, it is the *transparency of relations*. "You know for sure that the amount in the contract will not change, there are no commissions, insurance, fines, penalties, fees. Whereas conventional bank credit agreements include commissions for SMS notification, credit application review, life insurance, property insurance, and other required payments given usually in small print", — cited the owner of one of the Islamic financial companies as an example. "The contract for Islamic financing of this company consists of only one page, and what is more, it does not "use debt collectors' services'. Second, it is *a fairer distribution of risks*: "there are fewer risks for the borrower, since some of the risks are redistributed to the bank". Third, these are *milder consequences for borrowers who find themselves in an unexpected situation*. "The approaches of a conventional bank and an Islamic bank will be radically different: the Islamic bank does not charge fines for delay," one of the interviewed experts stressed. Fourth, it is *a fixed and non-changing cost of capital*.

The way of practical implementation of Islamic Finance advantages were described by the head of an Islamic Finance company using the example of the murabaha instrument: "First we buy a car, then we perform a full inspection of the supplier and the car ourselves. Then we resell this car to the customer. This applies to any product, property, real estate, etc. We express commitment to solve many problems for our clients whereas a conventional bank's main focus is collecting the money, so each credit agreement contains penalties for delay. Entrepreneurs often receive bank notifications warning about the rate increase, which makes them try to pay off ahead of time. High financial pressure under which businesses have to operate is further aggravated by various fines. In some situations, this can lead to disastrous results. This is especially evident in times of crisis and destroys many businesses. Islamic banking is free from this. Another important thing is price fixing. As soon as a deal is completed the price stays fixed, whereas a conventional bank can unilaterally change the interest rate under any loan agreement. We never change the terms, it is forbidden under Shariah law".

Another respondent, the head of a consulting company, summarized more broadly: "there is certain logic underneath Islamic Finance: the need to participate in business, in risks, and gaining more responsibility in investing. Unlike a consumer loan it can't be spent on idle purposes such as restaurants. Islamic Finance works in a different way. It requires a more specific connection with actions: buying a product, investing in a business, etc. It is just a more responsible investment system. <...> In conventional finance, the source of funds is not related to the subject of financing. Islamic finance is a more conservative approach to project selection. It involves an element of cooperation, an element of mutual control, and mutual responsibility".

In general, to quote the experts interviewed, "there are no restrictions on the rate of return in Islamic Finance itself", and it really "can be expensive if you create barriers for it'. The figures given by the experts are even more eloquent about the demand for Islamic financial services: e.g., according to the owner of one of the Islamic financial companies, the number of return clients who appreciated the advantages of Islamic Finance is more than 60%.

TARGET AUDIENCE OF ISLAMIC FINANCE IN RUSSIA

This section will discuss the demand for Islamic financial services by businesses and the population. What is the target audience of Islamic financial companies in Russia? Are they Muslims or representatives of other religions? If they are Muslims, how strictly do they adhere to the norms of Islam?

As for the demand for Islamic Finance, it was unanimously confirmed by all the experts. "Demand and understanding have grown significantly over the past years and are at a qualitatively different level," the respondents say.

As for the target audience of Islamic Finance, "the strategic target is 20–25 mln Muslims" living in Russia. One expert noted that "as soon as people learn about Islamic financial services, they try to use them instead of conventional ones. It is unclear whether consumers are in a situation of compulsion, and this is not very good from the point of view of self-perception. The state should strive to ensure equal access to services that correspond to the internal beliefs of citizens".

The head of an Islamic Finance company stressed: "We cannot say that Islamic Finance is only meant for Muslims. We see this in our practice. Our clients are not all observant Muslims. It's just more convenient for many people to work with us. We had Eastern Orthodox clients who sought for the absence of usury <...> 20% of our clients are non-observant Muslims or not Muslims at all". The head of another Islamic financial company noted that non-Muslims make up 10 to 15% of his company's clients.

When asked about the demand for Islamic Finance in the corporate and retail sectors, one of the respondents expressed an important idea: "businesses in Russia are in high need of financing, but they are usually satisfied with any financing <...> Business has no need for the allocation of resources. They usually need money for development, i.e. they are borrowers, so the source of money is the population <...> People would be more interested in Islamic Finance than businesses. For an individual, this [Islamic Finance] means new instruments, new opportunities". The majority of respondents confirmed that "Islamic Finance is for those who are not comfortable with the existing instruments". However, today alternatives exist only for those "who invest funds (e.g., in the stock market), but if you attract financing there are practically no alternatives". As for the size of the target businesses, respondents believe that Islamic Finance is "not particularly needed by large businesses", it is rather meant for small and medium-sized businesses. Thus, from the point of view of experts, the target audience of Islamic Finance here is the population, micro, small and medium-sized businesses.

FACTORS LIMITING THE DEVELOPMENT
OF THE ISLAMIC FINANCE MARKET IN RUSSIA

In this set of questions, we discussed what limits the practical development of Islamic Finance. is the lack of legislation really a preventing factor for potential investors? What, besides legislation, is important for the efficient development of this financial services sector in Russia?

Lack of special legislation and regulatory environment was recognized as a restricting factor for the development of the Islamic Finance sector by all the experts. The majority of the respondents believe that "market growth requires effort on the part of the Central Bank to build a system". One of the interviewees who has experience of joint projects with the Islamic Development Bank in Russia and abroad, says that "not a single country in the world began to develop Islamic Finance without a legal framework". He continues: "For them [Islamic investors] Russia is a hardly accessible territory <...> the Islamic Development Bank will never be proactive on territories with no political solution to this issue, this bank avoids any aggressive policy to promote Islamic Finance <...> the Islamic Development Bank begins to work only where there is a legal framework". He gives a rather vivid analogy: "in the 1990s, Western banks came here [to Russia] because there was a market that accepted their terms". Similarly, the Russian authorities should take some action if they intend to work with Islamic capital.

The head of one of the Islamic financial companies says that they are forced to "work not as a bank, but as a quasi-banking structure. All organizations like ours work according to their own schemes and formats", the owner of another added that "there is no suitable organizational and legal form for the work of an Islamic financial organization", the head of the third one noted that "now we need to come up with complex structures". However, some experts see their own advantages in this state of affairs: "We can work without regulation from the Central Bank. And this is an advantage because it is still unknown if the Central Bank decision-makers will possess the necessary knowledge and experience, and what decisions they will make <...> So far, it's even scary to think about it. But the downside is that it restricts investors".

The second important factor was identified by the respondents as the *"lack of a principal"*, or *"big and serious players"* in the market of Islamic financial services. "Serious players always stick to the legal field" to avoid potential risks. The heads of Islamic financial branches of conventional Russian banks see this as the cause of "serious restrictions and limits on Islamic financial transactions" they are facing.

The third factor, according to the experts, is *lack of knowledge.* According to one expert, Russians have "only basic knowledge about Islam". According to another respondent, "people have finally begun to understand that Islamic Finance is not about access to free money".

"The insufficient level of knowledge translates into the insufficient level of practice, namely the practice of active demand. Although the demand is actually growing, both the demand and the level of understanding have grown over these 10 years significantly", explains the third expert. As "the demand for Islamic Finance is growing along with education" the market itself, among other things, "requires investment in education".

The fourth factor revealed in the survey was "*the complexity of integrating the Islamic banking system into the usurious one*". Some experts pointed out that "conventional banks can't make Islamic fairness to their advantage". In their opinion, the Central Bank and the banking lobby are "actively promoting usury policy", and "there are no alternatives for the average person". One of the respondents explains: "Whereas in the conventional system one partner may be profiting while the other is losing, the Islamic system is free from it. If you are a partner, you are a partner in the true sense of the word. This is the new approach to money, partnership, interaction, and risk" offered by the Islamic financial doctrine.

The fifth factor was identified by the respondents as *professional training*. An expert who has worked for a long time in South-East Asia noted that "in Malaysia, all [the development of Islamic Finance] began with professional training of specialists". Another expert noted:" Developing an Islamic banking retail needs specialists whose professional training will take time".

MODEL OF INTRODUCTION OF ISLAMIC FINANCE IN THE RUSSIAN ECONOMY

At the end of the interview, we tried to understand how the respondents envisage further development of the Islamic Finance industry in Russia. What, in their opinion, is required for this sector of the financial market to occupy a significant niche.

One of their experts noted: "After the 2008 crisis, there was a certain hope that Russia would really start considering Islamic Finance as an alternative and supplement to the existing system. But then the Russian Direct Investment Fund was created and it became clear that dealing with Arabians is possible without Islamic Finance".

The practice of attracting foreign Islamic capital to Russia is represented by sporadic deals that "can be concluded within the current legislation". According to one expert, "it doesn't take any extra effort to arrange a couple of Islamic Finance deals for the corporate sector: accepting money is not a problem. Lawyers will find a lot of solutions, but it is much more difficult to implement Islamic Finance for the population: to do this, we need to create parallel regulation of the banking sector". He is convinced that Islamic Finance is "not a thing that will work on its own, so that the invisible hand of the market takes it and does everything itself".

According to the general opinion of respondents, "the more the number and variety of products, the more the market evolves", "Islamic Finance is better at withstanding crises". According to the experts, "the market is developing, but evolutionarily, without any incentives", "the idea [by the Central Bank] is being ignored", and "the authorities fail to understand how this [creating conditions for Islamic financial companies] could be beneficial for the economy". In their opinion, a number of large banks are interested in Islamic Finance "only at the level of hype <...> while the population looks at it as an idea that meets their needs".

The respondents share doubts about the state of the investment climate in the country. One expert put it this way: "the overall business environment in Russia is lame. Not only Islamic Finance is facing problems, but also business in general <...> There are not enough incentives for development". Another respondent noted: "I would not expect external Islamic or non-Islamic investments in Russia simply because Islamic Finance is similar to conventional banking in terms of risk assessment, choice of currency and region of investment <...> The potential for the development of Islamic Finance is to attract money from the population. There will be no other sources of money. The player who creates clear and reliable conditions for attracting Islamic Finance will at least raise some additional money from the market". The third expert indicated: "Russia is closed: it does not depend on international capital markets. Even the issue of sovereign Eurobonds is just for the record because there is enough money inside the country".

Speaking about models for the development of Islamic Finance, one of the experts focuses on "live and self-regulated" capital markets: "you have to be enabled to issue your own sovereign sukuk to trade them in the Gulf markets. We need our own Islamic funds. We need an Islamic stock index that can be traded all over the world. It will create liquidity for Russian stocks and new investment demand for them. We need Islamic private equity and venture capital funds <...> for breakthrough growth, we need a capital market, and banks are developing evolutionarily". Another expert believes that "there is a hope for banking digitalization which will create the necessary space" for the new "generation that lives

94

online and does not watch TV at all". However, *the majority of respondents noted that the market "lacks liquidity"*, and the existing Islamic financial companies develop only at the expense of internal financing. "Islamic Finance will become cheaper and occupy a significant part of the market only when there is capital for development. There is a need in large investors which can be represented by banks, because they have an excess of liquidity. They don't know who to deal with, who to offer financial services to, whereas we do", said the head of one of the Islamic financial companies. The owner of a consulting company explained the problem of the Islamic financial services market as follows: "saying that it is impossible to engage in Islamic Finance in Russia is far from true. The existence of such companies as "Financial House "Amal', 'LaRiba', etc. speaks for itself. But their business is not being expanded due to lack of investment. If they had some major investor, they could provide cheaper products. But in Russia, until recently, most of the major players who tried to develop the topic of Islamic Finance had to begin their activities in a situation of quite serious financial difficulties: this is true for both Ellipse Bank and TatFondBank. It seemed more like a desperate attempt to raise funding somewhere else when other instruments were no longer working".

During the interview, all the experts pointed out that the market for Islamic Finance "lacks scale, and the scale is eliminated by lack of legislative framework". The majority of respondents agreed that "the development of Islamic Finance should take place 'inside', rather than 'outside'", *"the most realistic way is the emergence of a major player which will make everything else spin"*, "big financial investments will make the development significantly easier", "whereas small and medium-sized players will not change the situation in the short term" because it is "a fairly long process". According to the respondents, "if some major player does it and shows everyone, then others will see that it is possible to earn money in this market". However, such a player can only appear after "building the necessary regulatory framework", better "with some benefits for business". As a large investor, or the so-called "major player", the experts see a financial and industrial group or bank from the top 50 which "would like to take and develop this business investing in the promotion and development" of Islamic Finance in Russia.

So, in Russia, interest in the Islamic economy and finance has a strong social base, a 25-million Muslim population making the largest ethnicity in Europe. However, despite the fact that the history of Islamic Finance in Russia is quite diverse and begins in 1991, this segment has not reached a large scope and fails occupy a significant share of the financial market. Using a sociological approach to analyzing this problem, we tried to find out the causes and propose solution. We have identified factors that, from the experts' point of view, limit the development of the Islamic financial services sector in Russia, and include lack of regulatory environment and major players, lack of knowledge and qualified personnel, and the difficulty of integration into the existing financial system. In addition, we found out to what extent Islamic Finance is in demand and competitive in Russia. Respondents confirmed that "the demand exists and it is growing" both among businesses and among the population. This is due to the presence of such fundamental competitive advantages of Islamic Finance which, according to the experts, are transparency of relationships, a fairer distribution of risks, a fixed and non-changing cost of capital, and milder consequences for borrowers who find themselves in an emergency situation. According to the experts, the target audience of Islamic Finance in Russia are individuals who, on the one hand, are not satisfied with the existing financial products, and on the other hand, are believers and adhere to religious norms (not only Islam). In addition, the audience of Islamic Finance, according to respondents, is small and medium-sized businesses, while "large businesses do not particularly need it". Thus, the development of Islamic Finance industry will largely contribute to increasing the availability of financial resources and be of strategic importance for the development of small and medium-sized businesses, especially in the provinces. As for the model of introducing Islamic Finance into the Russian economy, the majority of respondents came to the conclusion that the market "does not have enough liquidity" to scale the business of Islamic financial companies. Islamic Finance will become even more competitive and may take a significant market share if a large investor, such as a bank or a financial and industrial group, possesses enough capital to develop this sector (Appendix D). However, a large investor needs to minimize legal risks, which can only be ensured by the adoption of legislation on Islamic Finance.

It would be appropriate to sum up the results of the survey by most convincing words of the respondents themselves: "Islamic Finance has clear perspectives for development. Its availability in the Russian market of financial services is a positive fact in itself. <...> But at the moment, the market of Islamic Finance is in an embryonic stage of development <...> However its prospects are promising. The question is, whether it will be used or not". However, "for a country where population growth is mainly due to Muslims, this direction should be started as soon as possible", our experts conclude.

CHAPTER 8.
INVESTMENT STRATEGY OF THE ISLAMIC DEVELOPMENT BANK IN POST-SOVIET CENTRAL ASIA AND TRANSCAUCASIA

After gaining sovereignty in the early 1990s, the six countries of post-Soviet Central Asia and Transcaucasia, which include Azerbaijan, Kazakhstan, Kyrgyzstan, Tajikistan, Turkmenistan, and Uzbekistan, was in economic decline for almost a decade. Due to the chronic lack of investment, almost the entire infrastructure of these young states — road, energy sector, and irrigation — fell into disrepair. In addition, the growing population of the region demanded new and modern infrastructure facilities in the field of medicine and education, and business looked for access to new markets.

It is well known that efficient infrastructure reduces transport costs and increases the intensity of trade (Limao, and Vinables, 2001), which, as a result, leads to an increase in real incomes of the population and sustainable economic growth of the country. And vice versa, poor infrastructure generates significant costs, both direct and indirect. The largest investors in the development of socio-economic infrastructure are such multilateral development banks as the World Bank, the European Bank for Reconstruction and Development, the Asian Development Bank, the Islamic Development Bank and others (Faure, etc., 2015).

The countries of Central Asia and Transcaucasia with the predominant Muslim identity of their population[1] joined the Organization of the Islamic Conference in the 1990s[2]. a multilateral development bank under this organization is the Islamic Development Bank (IDB). There are 57 shareholding member states of this bank, and its assets amount to more than $30 bln. The largest shareholders of the IDB are Saudi Arabia (23.5%), Libya (9.43%), Iran (8.25%) and Nigeria (7.66%). The bank has the highest credit rating: Aaa from Moody's and AAA from S&P and Fitch. For the IDB, the priority area of capital application is the social and economic infrastructure of the participating countries. The geographical focus is mostly on countries such as Bangladesh (the IDB invested $21.4 bln), Pakistan ($12.4 bln), Egypt ($12.2 bln), and Turkey ($11.7 bln), which together account for almost a third of the

---

[1] The region is home to more than 70 million Muslims (4% of the world's share).
[2] In 2011 it was renamed the Organization of Islamic Cooperation.

world's Muslim population. The IDB provides long-term concessional financing for up to 30 years and invests in accordance with Islamic financial principles (IDB, 2020).

As for the post-Soviet countries of Central Asia and Transcaucasia, their cumulative share in the bank's subscribed capital is 0.34% (Appendix B). According to our estimates, the bank's total investment in this region for the period from 1990 to 2020 amounted to $6.8 bln. Thus, the average size of a single deal is almost $18 mln. Having analyzed a broad empirical base consisting of 385 deals financed by the IDB in this region, ranging from the construction of Islamic schools (madrassas) to the construction of gas pipelines we draw the following patterns:

- *firstly,* the IDB provides concessional long-term financing for up to 25–30 years with up to 10 year grace period;
- *secondly,* the IDB often participates in deals in a consortium with other international development banks: the World Bank, the Asian Development Bank, the European Bank for Reconstruction and Development, and others;
- *thirdly,* the IDB engages members of the Arab Coordination Group in its deals: the Saudi Fund for Development, the OPEC Fund for International Development, the Abu Dhabi Fund for Development, and the Kuwait Fund for Arab Economic Development. This, on the one hand, allows to diversify risks between different investors of the project, on the other — to expand bilateral investment cooperation between the countries of the Gulf and Central Asia and Transcaucasia;
- *fourthly,* the condition for providing capital from the IDB is co-financing by the local government, including tax benefits and other mandatory payments to the country's budget;
- *fifth,* for the development of the Islamic Finance industry, the IDB has allocated more than $165 mln in the form of technical assistance for the development of necessary legislation, as well as financing of Islamic financial structures (banks, leasing companies, funds);
- *sixth,* one-third of all IDB investments are allocated in Turkmenistan, Tajikistan and Kyrgyzstan, and two-thirds — in Uzbekistan, Kazakhstan and Azerbaijan, which corresponds to the Muslim population of these countries;
- *seventh,* despite the presence of projects in the financial, industrial and agricultural sectors, the main part of the IDB's investments in this region is directed to financing the physical infrastructure of road construction, water supply, oil and gas transportation, energy sector, housing, telecommunications, waste processing, healthcare and education centers (Table 8.1).

Table 8.1. The IDB's investments in the infrastructure of post–Soviet Central Asia and Transcaucasia

Type of infrastructure	Total investment by the IDB, $ bln	Share in total investment, %	Number of the deals, pcs.	Average size of a deal, $ mln
Road construction	1.12	23	34	33
Water supply and irrigation	1.09	23	43	25
Oil and gas infrastructure	0.74	16	3	247
Electricity infrastructure	0.48	10	18	27
Real estate and housing construction	0.45	9.5	8	56
Telecom	0.29	6	2	145
Healthcare infrastructure	0.22	5	24	9
Waste processing	0.20	4	1	200
Educational infrastructure	0.16	3.5	31	5
Total	4.75	100	164	29

Source: based on Appendix C.

Let's look at the latest trend in detail. 70% of the IDB's investments (which is almost $4.8 bln) was directed to financing the economic and social infrastructure of the region.

As the data in Table 8.1 shows, most of the funds were invested in *road construction* projects (23% of all infrastructure investments of the IDB in the region, or $1.12 bln). The largest projects were implemented in Kazakhstan — the construction of the 66-km Big Almaty Ring road ($100 mln) and the reconstruction of the 58-km road 'Border of South Kazakhstan region–Taraz' ($170 mln). Both of the sections are key segments of the Western Europe–Western China transit corridor. Co-investors of the IDB were the International Bank for Reconstruction and Development, the Asian Development Bank and the European Bank for Reconstruction and Development. The second project was continued with the reconstruction of 199-km Araz, Talas, Suusamyr, Kyrgyzstan Road, connecting Kazakhstan with the center of Kyrgyzstan. The IDB invested more than $33 mln in the project. In addition, the development of the region's railway infrastructure required $388 mln of IDB funds, which were allocated for the construction of the International North–South Transport Corridor that connects Kazakhstan, Turkmenistan and Iran. This railway was intended to enhance trade in the region.

The IDB invested $1.09 bln (23% of the total value) in the *water supply and irrigation infrastructure* sector. The largest number of projects (43 pcs.) were financed in this sphere, mainly in Azerbaijan and Uzbekistan. For example, the reconstruction of the Samur-Absheron irrigation channel in Azerbaijan, which was built in 1939–1940 using the Soviet method of people's construction. The project cost $50 mln, of which $10 mln was allocated by the IBD, $18 mln — by the Saudi Fund for Development, $8 mln — by the OPEC Fund for International Development, and $6.5 mln — by the government of Azerbaijan. In addition, the IDB invested heavily in the construction of an irrigation system in Tajikistan, which is rich in water resources. The project that received the most funding from the IDB was the Dangara valley irrigation system. The co-investors of the IDB, which invested more than $50 mln in the project, were the Kuwait Fund for Arab Economic Development ($4 mln) and the government of Tajikistan. a similar project was launched in Khatlon region of Tajikistan in 2019. Its value is $53.5 mln, and the investors are the IDB — $15 mln and a number of members of the Arab Coordination Group (the Saudi Fund for Development — $25 mln and the OPEC Fund for International Development — $10 mln), the share of the government of t Tajikistan is $3.5 mln.

The IDB invested $742 mln in the region's *oil and gas infrastructure*, of which $700 mln was received by Turkmenistan for the implementation of the TAPI interregional gas pipeline connecting Turkmenistan, Afghanistan, Pakistan and India.

The IDB has invested more than $479 mln in the development of the region's *electricity infrastructure*, and Azerbaijan received almost half of this amount for the construction of the 780 MW Janub Gas Turbine Power Plant with a total cost of almost 700 mln euros, where the Asian Development Bank invested 80% of the project cost. The IDB provided Islamic financing istisna (a contract for the future supply of a manufactured or constructed asset, often used by Islamic investors to finance construction and production) in the amount of $191 mln, and the OPEC Fund for International Development — 34 mln euros. a similar but smaller project — the reconstruction of the Mingechaur Thermal Power Plant in Azerbaijan — was funded in 1998. That time, the IDB invested $12.7 mln, and the European Bank for Reconstruction and Development — $21.65 mln. Speaking about the energy infrastructure sector, we should mention the international project CASA-1000, which is designed to transfer 1,300 MW of electricity from Kyrgyzstan and Tajikistan to Pakistan and Afghanistan via high-voltage power lines with a length of more than 1,200 km. The World Bank's contribution to the project was equal to half of its cost ($526.5 mln). The IDB invested more than $46 mln in the Kyrgyz part of the project and $70 mln in the Tajik part. In addition, the Tajik government received financing from the European Bank for Reconstruction and Development ($110 mln), the European Investment Bank ($70 mln), and the governments of Great Britain and Australia. The official launch of the CASA-1000 was given in 2016, and it is planned to be completed in 2020–2021.

The IDB allocated $450 mln to *real estate and housing construction* in the region. First of all, it was a project to finance a large-scale housing construction program in rural areas of Uzbekistan, where 75,000 standard modern individual residential buildings will be built by 2021. The total size of the program is $2.7 bln. Since 2012, it has been funded by the Asian Development Bank for a total of $500 mln. In addition, the project was invested by the IDB which allocated more than $400 mln in three tranches in the form of istisna. The IDB's partners in the Arab Coordination Group — the Saudi Fund for Development ($110 mln in three tranches) and the Kuwait Fund for Arab Economic Development ($30 mln) — also invested in the project.

In the *telecommunications sector*, the IDB has financed two projects in Turkmenistan totaling $288 mln. These investments were preceded by the withdrawal of the MTS Russian telecommunications company from the market at the end of 2017. It is planned to build 5G networks, a data center, and so on with the funds raised from the IDB.

More than $200 mln was invested in the development of *healthcare infrastructure*, of which almost half was allocated to the projects in Uzbekistan — the refurbishment of sanitary laboratories ($20 mln), oncological centers ($37 mln) and ambulance service ($24 mln). In addition, the 'Improving the Quality of Medical Services for Mothers and Children in 4 districts of Khatlon Region' Program was implemented in Tajikistan at the expense of the IDB. In 2019 it amounted to almost $27 mln, of which $23 mln was the funds of the IDB, one-third provided in the form of a grant and two-thirds in the form of returnable Islamic financing for a period of 20 years.

Due to the IDB's investment of almost $200 mln, a waste-processing infrastructure was built in Azerbaijan in 2010. It is the largest environmentally friendly incineration plant with a capacity of

500,000 tons per year, which is located near the previously existing open burial ground near Baku. At the expense of the IDB, specialized equipment was purchased according to the istisna Shariah standard for a period of 18 years (including a 3-year grace period). The incineration process generates 231.5 mln kWh of electricity per year, which is sent to the city grid to power 50,000 homes, and the ash and slag are used to produce asphalt. Before its construction, 80% of all household waste generated in Baku was sent for open burial. That caused serious environmental threats.

The IDB has invested over $150 mln in the region's *educational infrastructure*. Besides madrassas that were completely destroyed during the Soviet period, the funds were also directed to the development of general education institutions in Uzbekistan and Tajikistan. In Tajikistan the educational sector faced significant difficulties due to the physical damage caused by the civil unrest in 1992–1997 and the reduction in funding as a result of the economic downturn in the 1990s. The IDB has invested about $78 mln in this sector over a long-term period (25 years on average). Schools built in 13 districts of the country at the expense of the IDB are designed to train 12,000 children and employ 1,300 teachers.

Summing up, it should be noted that the IDB, along with other multilateral development banks, is a source of long-term concessional capital for the countries of Central Asia and Transcaucasia. Herewith, the IDB's investment strategy in this region is well diversified: no industry or project accounts for more than 25% of the total investment of this development bank. The countries of post-Soviet Central Asia and Transcaucasia, thanks to their membership in the Organization of Islamic Cooperation and its main financial institution — the Islamic Development Bank — attracted almost $7 bln in investment, as well as additional capital from members of the Arab Coordination Group, and implemented large-scale infrastructure development, which is one of the main factors for sustainable economic growth of states. In addition, the institutional development of the Islamic Finance industry is carried out in the study region through financial support from the IDB.

CONCLUSION

*All the forces in the world are not so powerful
as an idea whose time has come.*
Victor Hugo

The detailed presentation of the facts allowed us to make an objective analysis and obtain interesting scientific results:

- *first,* we found out that Islamic Finance in the post-Soviet Central Asia and Transcaucasia region accounts for more than $10 bln in investments, more than 1,000 transactions, and more than 20 Islamic financial organizations. We should note that the presence of Islamic Finance is gradually becoming more visible;
- *second,* development institutions still play an important role in the development of Islamic Finance practices. Thus, the main source of attracting Islamic Finance is still represented by investments of the Islamic Development Bank group, while private investment still occupies a small market share;
- *third,* it becomes clear that despite the growing external investments of the above mentioned group of the Islamic Development Bank, Islamic Finance needs to be developed 'from the inside', and for this, the ideals of Islamic Finance must be perceived and understood by the local population;
- *fourth,* we came to realization of high importance of the role of education of potential suppliers and consumers of Islamic financial services as well as the authorities in the development of this industry;
- *fifth,* we have found that Islamic Finance in each country develops in its own way: in Kazakhstan, for example, this development occurs 'from above' as part of state policy, and in Russia, it is mostly 'from below'. In Kazakhstan, Islamic Finance is developed through the corporate sector whereas in Kyrgyzstan it develops through microfinance services to the population. While Uzbekistan is just opening up to the ideas of Islamic Finance, Azerbaijan has actually cut itself off from them completely;
- *sixth,* the Islamic financial system in the CIS countries does not develop in vacuum, but is a reflection of the environment in which it exists and evolves;

- *seventh,* the market of Islamic financial services in the CIS countries, having passed the first stage of its development, is moving to the second, in which access to long-term funding becomes crucial both through attracting large investors and through the development of Islamic capital markets (sukuk and tawarruq).

Our analysis has shown that over the past three decades, Islamic Finance, having come a way that was neither easy nor rapid, is gradually taking root in the local financial practices. But while institutions as a framework can be built within a few years, then practice and culture can only be built over decades.

We have seen that the construction of the Islamic financial industry is a long and gradual trend. But like any major historical process, once started it goes to live for centuries.

We realized that Islamic Finance, taking its ideological roots in the Quran and the Sunnah of the prophet Muhammad, is completely modern in its professional approach. By reducing risks at any level from family to the state, Islamic Finance increases the availability of financial resources for businesses and the public, which provides great benefits for the entire economy.

Turning a blind eye to the extremely successful examples of Islamic financial structures operating in the UAE, Malaysia and Bahrain, arguing against creating special legislation for Islamic Finance based on unconvincing and inappropriate reasons about the secularism of the state is evidently futile. After all, the authorities, for instance, express no objections to the mass purchase of machinery and equipment in Europe, which may lead to technological dependence on the West. It is time to finally recognize the diversity of society and the right of the local Muslim population to enjoy financial services appropriate to their inner convictions. Moreover, we must develop a deep understanding of how Islamic Finance works because sooner or later we will have to address the problems of social injustice and marginalization of the society in the face of restrictions on political and economic freedoms. And I really want to believe that the next Chapter in the history of Islamic Finance will be written here, in the post-Soviet area.

REFERENCES

1. Aliyev, F. (2012). *The Politics of Islamic Finance in Central Asia and South Caucasus*. Available at: https://centralasiaprogram.org/archives/7679 Accessed May 2020.
2. Asian Development Bank (2012). *Turkmenistan — Afghanistan — Pakistan — India Natural Gas Pipeline Project*. Available at: https://www.adb.org/sites/default/files/project-document/73061/44463-013-reg-tar.pdf Accessed February 2020.
3. Asian Development Bank (2016a). *Asian Development Outlook 2016: Asia's Potential Growth*. Available at: https://www.adb.org/sites/default/files/publication/182221/ado2016.pdf Accessed May 2020.
4. Asian Development Bank (2016b). *Tajikistan, 2016–2020, Sector Assessment (Summary): Finance*. Available at: https://www.adb.org/sites/default/files/linked-documents/cps-taj-2016-2020-sd-01.pdf Accessed April 2020.
5. Asian Development Bank (2017). *Turkmenistan. Country Operations Final Review Validation, 2002–2016*. Available at: https://www.adb.org/sites/default/files/evaluation-document/365111/files/in360-17.pdf Accessed February 2020.
6. Aslan, R. (2019). *No god but God: The Origins, Evolution, and Future of Islam*. Azbooka Publishing House. (In Russian).
7. Axelrod, R. (1976). *Structure of Decision: The Cognitive Maps of Political Elites*. Princeton Legacy Library.
8. Bekkin, R. (2007). Islamic Economy: Between Capitalism and Socialism. *Voprosy Ekonomiki*. (10):147–155. https://doi.org/10.32609/0042-8736-2007-10-147-155 Accessed June 2020. (In Russian).
9. Bekkin, R. (2009). Islamic Finances in Azerbaijan. *Problemy sovremennoi ekonomiki*. No.1 (29):307–310. (In Russian).
10. Bekkin, R. (2010). Islamic Economic Model nowadays. Marjani, Moscow. (In Russian).
11. Chokaev, B. (2015). Islamic Finance: Opportunities for the Russian Economy. *Voprosy Ekonomiki*. (6):106–127. https://doi.org/10.32609/0042-8736-2015-6-106-127 Accessed June 2020. (In Russian).
12. European Bank for Reconstruction and Development (2018). *Uzbekistan Diagnostic. Assessing Progress and Challenges in Unlocking the Private Sector's Potential and Developing a Sustainable Market Economy*. 24 p.

13. Faure, R., etc. (2015). *Multilateral Development Banks: a short guide.* Available at: https://www.odi.org/sites/odi.org.uk/files/odi-assets/ publications-opinion-files/10098.pdf Accessed May 2020.
14. Gait, A. and Worthington A. (2007). *a Primer on Islamic Finance: Definitions, Sources, Principles and Methods.* Available at: https:// ro.uow.edu.au/cgi/viewcontent.cgi?article=1359&context=commpape rs Accessed January 2020.
15. Gottschalk, P. and Greenberg G. (2008). *Islamophobia: making Muslims the enemy.* Lanham, Rowman and Littlefield Publishers, Inc.
16. Hasan M., and Dridi J. (2010). *The Effects of the Global Crisis on Islamic and Conventional Banks: a Comparative Study.* Available at: https://www. imf.org/external/pubs/ft/wp/2010/wp10201.pdf Accessed June 2020.
17. Hoggarth, D. (2016). The rise of Islamic finance: post-colonial market building in central Asia and Russia. *International Affairs.* 92 (1): 115–136. https://doi.org/10.1111/1468-2346.12508
18. Holzhacker, H. and Skakova, D. (2019). *Kyrgyz Republic Diagnostic.* 36 p. (European Bank for Reconstruction and Development).
19. International Monetary Fund (2016). *Islamic Banking and Finance. Opportunities across Medium, Small and Medium Enterprises in the Kyrgyz Republic.* Available at: https://www.ifc.org/wps/wcm/connect/ f0c4b023-2361-43f8-82de-95ce39f0a0a3/Islamic+Banking+_KR_ Eng_Web.pdf?MOD=AJPERES&CVID=lblxMdd Accessed July 2020.
20. International Monetary Fund (2019). *Kyrgyz Republic.* IMF Country Report No. 19/208. 81 p.
21. International Monetary Fund (2019). *Republic of Uzbekistan: 2019 Article IV Consultation — Press Release and Staff Report.* IMF Country Report No. 19/129. 94 p.
22. Islamic Development Bank (2020). *Investor Presentation.* Available at: https://www.isdb.org/sites/default/files/media/documents/2020-02/ IsDB%20Investor%20Presentation%20(Feb%202020).pdf Accessed July 2020.
23. Islamic Finance Services Board (2018). *Islamic Financial Services Industry Stability Report 2018.* 163 p.
24. Kalimullina, M. (2010). Sociocultural factors in the national model of Russian Economy (the evidence from sociological research on Islamic Economy and Finance amoung the population Russia and CIS countries). *Economy. Entrepreneurship. Environment.* Vol.2, No.24, pp.13–20. (In Russian).
25. Lewis, B. (2017). *The Arabs in History.* Tsentrpoligraf, Moscow. (In Russian).

26. Limao, N. and Vinables A.J. (2001). *Infrastructure, Geographical Disadvantage, Transport Costs, and Trade.* Available at: http://documents1.worldbank.org/curated/en/662351468331778084/pdf/773650JRN020010aphical0Disadvantage.pdf Accessed May 2020.

27. Mauro, F., etc. (2013). *Islamic Finance in Europe.* Available at: https://www.ecb.europa.eu/pub/pdf/scpops/ecbocp146.pdf Accessed June 2020.

28. Ministry of Finance of the Republic of Tajikistan (2018). *Public Debt Report 2018.* Available at: http://minfin.tj/downloads/otchet_2018vd.pdf Accessed April 2020. (In Russian).

29. Nagimova, A. (2013). Arab capital in the Russian Federation. *Problemy sovremennoi ekonomiki.* No.3 (47):161−164. (In Russian).

30. Nagimova, A. (2018a). *Mutual Investment between CIS and GCC countries.* Infra-M, Moscow. https://doi.org/10.12737/monography_5984598c29bfc2.57551870 Accessed Decemner 2019. (In Russian).

31. Nagimova, A. (2018b). Raising Arab Capital: Experiences of Russian Regions. *Mirovaya ekonomika i mezhdunarodnye otnosheniya.* Vol. 62, No 2, pp. 57-61. https://doi.org/10.20542/0131-2227-2018-62-2-57-61 Accessed July 2020. (In Russian).

32. Nagimova, A. (2020). Arab Investments in Russian Infrastructure. *Mirovaya ekonomika i mezhdunarodnye otnosheniya.* Vol. 64, No 3, pp. 80-87. https://doi.org/10.20542/0131-2227-2020-64-3-80-87 Accessed July 2020. (In Russian).

33. National Bank of the Kyrgyz Republic (2019). *Annual report 2018.* Available at: https://www.nbkr.kg/DOC/27062019/000000000052567.pdf Accessed April 2020.

34. Pew Research Center (2015). *The Future of World Religions: Population, Growth Projections, 2010–2050.* Available at: https://assets.pewresearch.org/wp-content/uploads/sites/11/2015/03/PF_15.04.02_ProjectionsFullReport.pdf Accessed May 2020.

35. Skolkovo (2018). *The Islamic economy is the fastest growing large economy. Eurasian focus.* Available at: https://iems.skolkovo.ru/downloads/documents/SKOLKOVO_IEMS/Research_Reports/SKOLKOVO_IEMS_Research_2018-07-04_ru.pdf Accessed June 2020 (In Russian).

36. Thomson Reuters (2015). *Kazakhstan. a new frontier to Islamic Finance.* Available at: https://www.cibafi.org/Files/L1/Content/CI1637-KazakhstanCountryReport2015.pdf Accessed January 2020.

37. Transparency International (2019). *Corruption Perceptions Index 2019* Available at: https://www.transparency.org/cpi2019 Accessed February 2020.

38. USAID (2016). *Study for the leasing market operations of Kyrgyz Republic.* Available at: http://ub.kg/wp-content/uploads/2016/02/Issledovanie-rynka-lizingovyh-operatsij-KR_17-fevralya-2016.pdf Accessed April 2020. (In Russian).

39. Warde, I. (2000). *Islamic Finance in the Global Economy.* Edinburgh University Press, Edinburgh.

40. WEF (2017). *The Global Competitiveness Report 2017–2018.* Available at: http://www3.weforum.org/docs/GCR2017-2018/05FullReport/Th eGlobalCompetitivenessReport2017%E2%80%932018.pdf Accessed December 2019.

41. Wolters, A. (2013). *Islamic finance in the states of Central Asia: Strategies, institutions, first experiences.* Available at: https://www.pfh.de/fileadmin/ Content/PDF/forschungspapiere/islamic_finance_in_the_states_of_ central_asia_by_alexander_wolters.pdf Accessed February 2020.

42. Z/Yen (2019). *The Global Financial Centres Index.* Available at: https:// www.longfinance.net/media/documents/GFCI_26_Report_v1.0.pdf Accessed January 2020.

ABBREVIATIONS

ADB — the Asian Development Bank

EBRD — the European Bank for Reconstruction and Development

IDB — the Islamic Development Bank

IMF — the International Monetary Fund

OIC — the Organization of Islamic Cooperation

ICD — the Islamic Corporation for the Development of the Private Sector (part of IDB group)

ICIEC — the Islamic Corporation for the Insurance of Investment and Export Credit (part of IDB group)

IFTC — the International Islamic Trade Finance Corporation (part of IDB group)

DEFINITIONS

The Arab Coordination Group is an informal association of bilateral and multilateral development institutions in the Gulf countries.

Islamic Finance is a set of financial institutions and instruments that comply with Shariah (Islamic law).

Islamic banking is a banking system that is based on the Islamic financial principles.

Islamic window is a separate branch or department that operates within a conventional Bank and provides products and services in accordance with Islamic financial principles. The accounts and financial resources of the conventional Bank and the Islamic window should not be 'mixed'. The Islamic window allows conventional banks to expand the portfolio of banking products offered to businesses and the public without major additional investments, and at least reach customers who adhere to the norms of Islam.

Shariah Board is an independent body which confirms that operations comply with Islamic financing principles.

Sukuk is Islamic bond that represent the holder's right to a certain share of the profit generated by the asset over a certain period of time until maturity.

Ijarah — Islamic leasing.

Takaful — Islamic insurance.

Murabaha is one of the most widespread types of Islamic Finance consisting in the purchase of a product by a financial institution at the request of the client and the subsequent resale of this product to the client by installments with a pre-agreed and constant margin.

Mudaraba is equity type of Islamic financing, where one party provides capital, and the other manages the project, while the profits are distributed in a predetermined ratio, and the investor is responsible for losses.

Musharaka is a joint venture in which each party provides capital for its implementation, while the profits are distributed among the participants in proportion to their contribution, and the losses — according to the agreement of the parties.

Istisna is a long-term Islamic financial agreement for the construction or manufacture of some asset with an obligation to deliver them to the buyer upon completion. The advantage of istisna is that payments by the client can be made in installments, after delivery or completion of the project. .

Tawarruq is an Islamic financial agreement for the purchase of deferred payment and sale of the same product to a 3rd party at the spot price. It is used by many Islamic banks for liquidity management..

Wakala is an agency agreement under which an agent (wakeel) undertakes to manage the asset given to him in exchange for a certain reward (a lump sum or a share of the invested amount).

Qard-hasan is Islamic charity loan.

Wadiah yad dhamanah is Islamic financial agreement of safekeeping or guaranteed deposits.

APPENDIX A

KAZAKHSTAN

Population (2019):	18.6 mln
Muslim population (2020):	72%
GDP in current prices (2018):	$179 bln
GDP real change (2018–2019):	4.1%
GDP per head (PPP, 2019):	$28,510
Public debt/GDP (2017):	20.8%
Inflation rate (2019):	5.3%
Recorded unemployment (2019):	4.7%
Lending interest rate (2019):	12.8%
Gross national savings/ GDP (2017):	23.7%
Exports (2018):	$64.1 bln
Imports (2018):	$37.6 bln
Exports — commodities (2018):	Petroleum ($38.3 bln), gas ($3.13 bln), copper ($2.8 bln), ferroalloys ($2.26 bln), petroleum products ($2.26 bln), etc.
Exports — partners (2018):	Italy ($10.3 bln), China ($6.41 bln), Netherlands ($6.04 bln), Russia ($5.28 bln), France ($3.91 bln), etc.
Imports — commodities (2018):	Gas ($1.05 bln), petroleum products ($1.01bln), broadcasting equipment ($0.88 bln), medications ($0.87 bln), cars ($0.7 bln), etc.
Imports — partners (2018):	Russia ($13 bln), China ($8.71 bln), Germany ($1.71 bln), Italy ($1.35 bln), Uzbekistan ($1.22 bln), etc.

UZBEKISTAN

Population (2019):	33 mln
Muslim population (2020):	97.1%
GDP in current prices (2018):	$50.5 bln
GDP real change (2018–2019):	5.5%
GDP per head (PPP, 2019):	$7,580
Public debt/GDP (2017):	24.3%
Inflation rate (2019):	13.8%
Recorded unemployment (2019):	4.9%
Lending interest rate (2019):	—
Gross national savings/GDP (2017):	32.7%
Exports (2018):	$105 bln
Imports (2018):	$18.1 bln
Exports — commodities (2018):	Gold ($2.49 bln), gas ($2.45 bln), cotton ($0.73 bln), copper ($0.51 bln), polyethylen ($0.43 bln), etc.
Exports — partners (2018):	Switzerland ($2.48 bln), China ($2.24 bln), Russia ($1.64 bln), Kazakhstan ($1.22 bln), Turkey ($0.88 bln), etc.
Imports — commodities (2018):	Car components ($0.89 bln), medications ($0.66 bln), petroleum products ($0.5 bln), cars ($0.4 bln), spinning equipment ($0.4bln), etc.
Imports — partners (2018):	China ($3.78 bln), Russia ($3.33 bln), South Korea ($2.09 bln), Kazakhstan ($1.65 bln), Turkey ($1 bln), etc.

AZERBAIJAN

Population (2019):	10.1 mln
Muslim population (2020):	97.3%
GDP in current prices (2018):	$46.9 bln
GDP real change (2018–2019):	2.1%
GDP per head (PPP, 2019):	$18,660
Public debt/GDP (2019):	54.1%
Inflation rate (2019):	2.7%
Recorded unemployment (2019):	6.4%
Lending interest rate (2019):	14.3%
Gross national savings/ GDP (2017):	24.6%
Exports (2018):	$19.9 bln
Imports (2018):	$11.9 bln
Exports — commodities (2018):	Petroleum ($16.1 bln), gas ($1.52 bln), petroleum products ($524 mln), tomatoes ($177 mln), gold ($151 mln), etc.
Exports — partners (2018):	Italy ($5.99 bln), Turkey ($1.85 bln), Israel ($1.31 bln), Czech Republic ($954 mln), Germany ($820 mln), etc.
Imports — commodities (2018):	Gold ($1.29 bln), cars ($437 mln), pipes ($380 mln), gas ($313 mln), gas turbines ($282 mln), etc.
Imports — partners (2018):	Russia ($1.88 bln), Turkey ($1.55 bln), UK ($1.3 bln), China ($674 mln), Germany ($603 mln), etc.

TURKMENISTAN

Population (2019):	5.9 mln
Muslim population (2020):	93%
GDP in current prices (2018):	$40.8 bln
GDP real change (2018–2019):	3%
GDP per head (PPP, 2019):	$12,410
Public debt/GDP (2017):	28.8%
Inflation rate (2019):	15%
Recorded unemployment (2019):	–
Lending interest rate (2019):	15%
Gross national savings/ GDP (2017):	23.9%
Exports (2018):	$9.11 bln
Imports (2018):	$2.38 bln
Exports — commodities (2018):	Gas ($7.23 bln), petroleum products ($0.8bln), peat ($0.18 bln), cotton ($0.16 bln), raw cotton ($0.11 bln), etc.
Exports — partners (2018):	China ($7.3 bln), Afghanistan ($0.3 bln), Turkey ($0.26 bln), Uzbekistan ($0.23 bln), Georgia ($0.17 bln), etc.
Imports — commodities (2018):	Harvesting equipment ($98.8 bln), special-purpose ships ($89.3 mln), medications ($72.8 mln), steam turbines ($63 mln), pipes ($57.7 mln), etc.
Imports — partners (2018):	Turkey ($0.47 bln), China ($0.32 bln), Russia ($0.29 bln), UAE ($0.26 bln), Germany ($0.17 bln), etc.

KYRGYZSTAN

Population (2019):	6.2 mln
Muslim population (2020):	89.4%
GDP in current prices (2018):	$8.09 bln
GDP real change (2018–2019):	4.4%
GDP per head (PPP, 2019):	$4,220
Public debt/GDP (2019):	56%
Inflation rate (2019):	0.8%
Recorded unemployment (2019):	7.4%
Lending interest rate (2019):	19.4%
Gross national savings/ GDP (2017):	27.3%
Exports (2018):	$2.69 bln
Imports (2018):	$8.66 bln
Exports — commodities (2018):	Gold ($1.36 bln), ore minerals ($124 mln), copper scrap ($106 mln), woman's knitting ($94.2 mln), petroleum products ($87 mln), etc.
Exports — partners (2018):	UK ($1.32 bln), Russia ($387 mln), Kazakhstan ($354 mln), Uzbekistan ($143mln), Turkey ($104 mln), etc.
Imports — commodities (2018):	Petroleum products ($834 mln), rubber shoes ($632 mln), man's suits ($242 mln), cotton ($217 mln), knitted sweaters ($215 mln), etc.
Imports — partners (2018):	China ($4.55 bln), Russia ($1.68 bln), Kazakhstan ($680 mln), Turkey ($380 mln), Uzbekistan ($252 mln), etc.

TAJIKISTAN

Population (2019):	9.3 mln
Muslim population (2020):	96.4%
GDP in current prices (2018):	$7.52 bln
GDP real change (2018–2019):	3.7%
GDP per head (PPP, 2019):	$2,920
Public debt/GDP (2017):	50.4%
Inflation rate (2019):	7.6%
Recorded unemployment (2019):	—
Lending interest rate (2019):	29%
Gross national savings/ GDP (2017):	24.4%
Exports (2018):	$3.63 bln
Imports (2018):	$1.16 bln
Exports — commodities (2018):	Gold ($212 mln), aluminum ($181 mln), zinc ores ($166 mln), lead ores ($116 mln), copper ores ($75,2 mln), etc.
Exports — partners (2018):	Kazakhstan ($308 mln), Switzerland ($213mln), Turkey ($196 mln), Uzbekistan ($110 mln), Afghanistan ($83.2 mln), etc.
Imports — commodities (2018):	Petroleum products ($239 mln), gas ($161mln), wheat ($160 mln), aircrafts, helicopters ($108 mln), rubber shoes ($81.1 mln), etc.
Imports — partners (2018):	China ($1.43 bln), Russia ($849 mln), Kazakhstan ($522 mln), Turkey ($177 mln), Uzbekistan ($137 mln), etc.

RUSSIA

Population (2019):	148.9 mln
Muslim population (2020):	11.4%
GDP in current prices (2018):	$1.66 bln
GDP real change (2018–2019):	1.2%
GDP per head (PPP, 2019):	$28,120
Public debt/GDP (2017):	15.5%
Inflation rate (2019):	4.5%
Recorded unemployment (2019):	4.7%
Lending interest rate (2019):	9%
Gross national savings/ GDP (2017):	26.5%
Exports (2018):	$427 bln
Imports (2018):	$231 bln
Exports — commodities (2018):	Petroleum ($134 bln), petroleum products ($77.5 bln), gas ($27.4 bln), coal ($18.9 bln), wheat ($10.7 bln), etc.
Exports — partners (2018):	China ($55.2 bln), Netherlands ($41 bln), Germany ($23.3 bln), Belarus ($21.6 bln), Italy ($18.9 bln), etc.
Imports — commodities (2018):	Cars ($10.2 bln), car components ($8.26 bln), medications ($8.01 bln), broadcasting equipment ($6.9 bln), aircrafts, helicopters, and rockets ($5.39 bln), etc.
Imports — partners (2018):	China ($45.4 bln), Germany ($30.8 bln), Беларусь ($12.6 bln), Italy ($8.97 bln), USA ($8.78 bln), etc.

Source: based on the data of The Economist Intelligence Unit, the Central Intelligence Agency, the Pew Research, and the Observatory of Economic Complex

APPENDIX B

Islamic Development Bank in the post–Soviet Central Asia and Transcaucasia

Country	OIC membership year	IDB membership year	Total investment, $ mln	Number of deals, pcs.	Average size of a deal, $ mln	% Total Capital	Capital Subscription, $ mln
Uzbekistan	1996	2003	1,990	103	19.3	0.03	13.4
Kazakhstan	1995	1995	1,453	87	16.7	0.11	54
Turkmenistan	1992	1994	1,449	15	96.6	0.01	5
Azerbaijan	1992	1992	1,118	66	17	0.1	50.9
Tajikistan	1992	1996	488	64	7.6	0.04	18.2
Kyrgyzstan	1992	1993	324	50	6.5	0.05	25.8
Total	–	–	6,782	385	17.6	0.34	167.3

Source: based on the data of the Islamic Development Bank and Appendix C.

APPENDIX C

THE IDB DEALS IN KAZAKHSTAN

Name	Summary	Status	Period	Size of investment
	Finance			
Zaman Leasing LLP	Zaman Leasing LLP Sector: Finance (Trade (Murabaha))	Active	Jul 2017 — Mar 2018	$2,500,000
Kazakhstan Ijarah Company (NBFI)	Kazakhstan Ijarah Company (NBFI) Sector: Finance (Trade (Murabaha))	Active	Dec 2019 — Dec 2019	$67,359,551
KazAgroFinance	KazAgroFinance Sector: Finance (Trade (Murabaha))	Active	Sept 2019 — Dec 2019	$13,650
Zaman Bank	Zaman Bank Sector: Finance (Equity)	Active	Aug 2019 — Dec 2019	$27,000
Kazakhstan Global Line (Sukuk)	Kazakhstan Global Line (Sukuk) Sector: Finance (Trade (Murabaha))	Active	Aug 2019 — Dec 2019	$56,000
T.A. for the Development of an Islamic Finance Master Plan for the Republic of Kazakhstan	To assist AIFC in developing an Islamic Finance Master Plan for Kazakhstan	Active	Jul 2018 — Dec 2019	$270,000
KazAgroFinance	KazAgroFinance Sector: Finance (Trade (Murabaha))	Active	Sep 2015 — Mar 2018	$25,000,000
Zaman Leasing LLP	Zaman Leasing LLP Sector: Finance (Trade (Murabaha))	Active	Nov 2013 — Mar 2018	$12,000,000
Zaman Bank	Zaman Bank Sector: Finance (Equity)	Active	Dec 2012 — Mar 2018	$10,000,000
AIC Investment	AIC Investment Sector: Finance (Trade (Murabaha))	Active	Nov 2012 — Mar 2018	$10,000,000

Name	Summary	Status	Period	Size of investment
Kazakhstan Leasing Company	Kazakhstan Leasing Company Sector: Finance (Equity)	Active	Jul 2013 — Mar 2018	$10,000,000
Microfinance to Rural Areas Project	The project aims at contributing to the efforts of the Government to achieving economic growth and poverty alleviation through employment creation by providing appropriate and reliable microfinance services to the rural population with a focus on women and small scale agrarian farmers. The project will help the rural population start new businesses and expand on current ones as also introducing Shariah compliant microfinance services and products	Completed	Jun 2011 — Oct 2014	$10,150,757
Kazagrofinance line of financing	The main Objective is to enhance production capacity of Kazakhstan farmers, which is in line of Jeddah Declaration	Completed	Sept 2009 — Dec 2011	$30,000,000
Nurbank line of financing	The main objective is to enhance production capacity of Kazakhstan farmers, which is in line of Jeddah Declaration	Completed	Sept 2009 — Dec 2011	$10,000,000
All Goods Acceptable Under ITFC Rules for Trade Financing	All Goods Acceptable Under ITFC Rules for Trade Financing Sector: Finance (Trade (Murabaha))	Completed	Jan 2009 — Mar 2018	$5,000,000
Kazkommerts-bank	The main objectives of the proposed line of financing to Kazkommertsbank are (i)provide access to longer term funds (ii) contribute to economic growth through increased lending to SMEs	Completed	Dec 2007 — May 2012	$50,000,000

Name	Summary	Status	Period	Size of investment
Halyk Bank	The objective of the proposed line of financing is to i) provide access to longer term funds, ii) contribute to economic growth	Completed	Aug 2007 — Apr 2013	$50,000,000
Limited Liabilities Co. «BOGVI»	Limited Liabilities Co. «BOGVI» Sector: Finance (Leasing)	Completed	Feb 2004 — Mar 2018	$,4,000,000
Project (UID 208)	Sector: Finance (Instalment Sale)	Completed	Apr 2000 — Mar 2018	$2,000,000
Agriculture				
Agriculture	Agriculture Sector: Finance (Leasing)	Active	Apr 2014 — Mar 2018	$9,000,000
Forum on the Role of the Integrated Agriculture Value Chains in Ensuring Food Security in the OIC MCs	Contribute to the Forum on «the Role of Integrated Agriculture Value Chains in Ensuring Food Security in the OIC MCs», 31 October 2018, Astana, Kazakhstan	Active	Oct 2018 — Dec 2019	$42,000
Training Program on "Applying Biotechnological Techniques in Field Crops Breeding" for Staff from Kazakhstan Ministry of Agriculture and National Management Holding	Construction of 2-storey school building	Completed	Oct 2017 — Oct 2017	$17,500
Wheat	Wheat Sector: Agriculture (Trade (Murabaha))	Completed	Dec 2014 — Mar 2018	$50,000,000
AIC Invest	AIC Invest Sector: Agriculture (Trade (Murabaha))	Active	Jul 2013 — Mar 2018	$10,000,000

Name	Summary	Status	Period	Size of investment
AIC Invest	AIC Invest Sector: Agriculture (Trade (Murabaha))	Active	Jul 2013 — Mar 2018	$10,000,000
Wheat	Wheat Sector: Agriculture (Trade (Murabaha))	Completed	Jun 2013 – Mar 2018	$50,000,000
Wheat	Wheat Sector: Agriculture (Trade (Murabaha))	Completed	May 2013 — Mar 2018	$125,000,000
Wheat	Wheat Sector: Agriculture (Trade (Murabaha))	Completed	Dec 2012 — Mar 2018	$50,000,000
Wheat	Wheat Sector: Agriculture (Trade (Murabaha))	Completed	Sep 2012 — Mar 2018	$65,000,000
Wheat	Wheat Sector: Agriculture (Trade (Murabaha))	Completed	Mar 2012 — Mar 2018	$30,000,000
Wheat	Wheat Sector: Agriculture (Trade (Murabaha))	Completed	Feb 2012 — Mar 2018	$65,000,000
Wheat	Wheat Sector: Agriculture (Trade (Murabaha))	Completed	Sep 2011 — Mar 2018	$50,000,000
Wheat	Wheat Sector: Agriculture (Trade (Murabaha))	Completed	Feb 2011 — Mar 2018	$50,000,000
AGRO TESS LLC	AGRO TESS LLC	Completed	Jun 2010 — Apr 2011	$528,611
AGRO TESS LLC	AGRO TESS LLC	Completed	May 2010 — April 2011	$430,000
SANDY RAIYMBEK LLC	SANDY RAIYMBEK LLC	Completed	Jun 2010 — Apr 2011	$300,000
Kazakh farmers production capacities	Kazakh farmers production capacities	Completed	Apr 2010 — Dec 2011	$29,911,672
Meat processing plant	Meat processing plant	Completed	Nov 2009 — Apr 2011	$5,900,000

Name	Summary	Status	Period	Size of investment
Flour production factory	Flour production factory	Completed	Nov 2009 - Dec 2012	$4,094,000
TSELINA INVEST. LLP	TSELINA INVEST. LLP	Completed	Oct 2009 — Apr 2011	$1,740,600
SHUISKOE-XXI LLP	SHUISKOE-XXI LLP	Completed	Jul 2009 — Apr 2011	$422,814
RODNIK PLUS LLP	RODNIK PLUS LLP	Completed	Oct 2008 — Apr 2011	$483,000
Agric. Products	Agric. Products Sector: Finance (Trade (Murabaha))	Completed	Mar 2003 — Mar 2018	$10,000,000
Agrofirma Kenozhi Ltd., Schuchinsk	Agrofirma Kenozhi Ltd., Schuchinsk Sector: Finance (Leasing)	Completed	Mar 2003 — Mar 2018	$5,157,000
Production cooperative (pc) «Tulkim LLP»	Production cooperative (pc) «Tulkim LLP»	Completed	Apr 2002 — May2015	$330,290
Production cooperative (pc) «Rodina»	Production cooperative (pc) «Rodina»	Completed	Jul 2001 — Mar 2012	$285,000
Joint stock co. «Balhashsut»	Joint stock co. «Balhashsut» for the con	Completed	Jul 2001 — May 2015	$330,000
Road construction				
Almaty Ring Road PPP (BAKAD) Project	The Project objective is financing, construction and operation of 66 km tolled PPP highway that will improve the quality of the transport services, reduce road accident rate, positively impact environment by lowering road congestion and ultimately contribute to economic and social development of Almaty city, Republic of Kazakhstan	Active	Jul 2019 — Oct 2019	$100,000,000

Name	Summary	Status	Period	Size of investment
Reconstruction of Road Section Border of South Kazakhstan Oblast-Taraz Project	The project is part of the Government's plan to upgrade and improve the road corridor linking Western Europe to Western China through Kazakhstan with the objective of improving transport efficiency and safety, and promote development along one of Kazakhstan's main strategic road transport corridors. The project output will be 58 kms of constructed highway sections in Zhambyl Oblast and improved road operation and maintenance system	Completed	Jul 2009 — Jan 2014	$169,999,999
F.S. and Preliminary Design for Baravoe-Kokshetau-Petropavlovsk Road Project	The T.A. is for preparing a Feasibility Studies and Preliminary Design for the Baravoe-Kokshetau-Petropavlovsk Road which consists of two lanes with asphalt pavement and carriageway of 15 m and design speed of 120 km/hr	Completed	Jul 2002 — May 2004	$232,100
Karaganda-Astana road project	The project aims at construct 183km of the Karaganda-Astana road which is part of the Almaty-Astana road (1204 km) the construction will increase the road transport efficiency	Completed	Feb 2000 — Aug 2005	$20,000,000
Reconstruction of the Almaty-Gulshad road	Reconstruct the last 88 km of the Almaty-Gulshad road which is part of the Almaty-Akmola road (1200 km) this construction will increase the road transport efficiency	Completed	May 1999 — Nov 2003	$9,369,500

Name	Summary	Status	Period	Size of investment
F.S. study for Karaganda-akmola road	To undertake F.S. of Karaganda-Akmola road based on the volume of future traffic, to survey and ascertain need for realignment/ reconstruction of sections of the road, the structures (bridges culverts)	Completed	Jun 1996 – Jun 2006	$181,875
T.A. for economic F.S. of Almaty-Bystrovka road	i) To undertake economic F.S. of the Almaty-Bystrovka road based on the volume of furture. ii)to estimate cost of building the uzunaghach_bystrovka portion of the road iii)to estimate the number and location of motels, services stations to be constructed along the road	Completed	Jul 1994 – Jun 2006	$170,759
Industry				
Diagnostic Mission to initiate a Reverse Linkage Project between Kazakhstan (Recipient) and Malaysia (Provider) in Halal Ecosystem	To undertake a peer-to-peer diagnostic study to assess the capacity development needs of the TRMC and accordingly identify/propose activities as well as solutions to address these gaps by transferring the knowledge and expertise of the three Malaysian Halal-related agencies	Completed	Oct 2016 – May 2017	$21,000
Wireline Oilfield Services	Wireline Oilfield Services, Sector: Industry & Mining (Instalment Sale)	Active	Aug 2016 – Mar 2018	$8,240,626
PREMIUM LOGISTICS LLP	PREMIUM LOGISTICS LLP	Completed	Nov 2011 – Jan 2013	$457,765
PREMIUM LOGISTICS LLP	PREMIUM LOGISTICS LLP	Completed	Nov 2011 – Jan 2012	$3,013,869
PREMIUM LOGISTICS LLP	PREMIUM LOGISTICS LLP	Completed	Nov 2011 – May 2015	$736,290
PREMIUM LOGISTICS LLP	PREMIUM LOGISTICS LLP	Completed	Nov 2010 – Apr 2011	$4,577,696
BRICK Products Co. LLP	BRICK Products Co. LLP	Completed	May 2009 – Apr 2011	$7,500,000
BIOKOM LLP	BIOKOM LLP	Completed	Apr 2009 – Apr 2011	$6,900,000

Name	Summary	Status	Period	Size of investment
Establishment of a Lab. for halal certification of food	The project aims at facilitate establishing a Lab. for halal certification of food and agriculture products to ensure proper analysis and quality certification of food and agri. products in the country	Completed	Sep 2008 — Apr 2011	$315,400
Electronic	Electronic Sector (Trade (Murabaha))	Completed	Feb 2004 — Mar 2018	$1,000,000
Oil Transp.	Oil Transp. Sector (Trade (Murabaha))	Completed	Feb 2004 — Mar 2018	$10,000,000
Purch. of Fiber Optic Cables &Acsries CJSC	Purch. of Fiber Optic Cables &Acsries CJSC Sector: Finance (Trade (Murabaha))	Completed	Feb 2004 — Mar 2018	$15,000,000
	Water supply			
Rehabilitation of Irrigation and Drainage	The development objective is to enhance agriculture productivity and production and increase farmers' income and welfare of the rural community, by improving water use efficiency and timely water delivery, improving soil fertility, maintaining the groundwater table and reducing the salinity	Active	Sep 2017 — Dec 2019	$143,000,000
Developing a Reverse Linkage Sub-Project between Kazakhstan and United Arab Emirates on "Developing the Capacities of the Water Resources Committee, Kazakhstan"	Raising the capacity of the Water Resources Committee, Kazakhstan in managing the salinity of soil as well as using Geographical Information System (GIS) system for optimizing the utilization of water and soil	Active	Mar 2017 — Dec 2019	$9,700

Name	Summary	Status	Period	Size of investment
Rural Water Supply Project	The project aims at improving the health and quality of life of rural population of the Karaganda Oblast, through provision of safe and easy access to drinking water services. It includes civil works, equipment, detailed design and project supervision consultancy, project management, etc.	Completed	Sep 2003 — Mar 2010	$9,596,299
Kokshetau mineral water CO LTD.	Kokshetau mineral water CO LTD.	Completed	Dec 2001 — May 2015	$1,072,000
R&D				
Developing the Capacity of Al-Farabi Kazakh National University, Kazakhstan in Phytochemical Development	The project's objective will be achieved through supporting the KazNU in creating a critical mass of qualified researchers in phytochemical development, and complementing its infrastructure with the necessary chemicals and equipment	Active	Jul 2016 — Dec 2019	$150,000
Eighth Int'l Conference on Solid State Physics of a Firm Body, Almaty, Kazakhstan: 23-26 Aug 2004	The conference will bring solid state physics experts and scientists to share experience, take stock of new S&T advancements, enhance S&T cooperation and strengthen individual and cooperative science_base in this important field, including applications to new materials, resources_saving technologies, treatment of waste products from industry and nuclear facilities	Completed	Aug 2004 — Jan 2005	$30,000
C.B. of the Institute of Physics and Technology	The T.A. aims at capacity building of the Institute with a view to strengthening its research center through procuring appropriate equipment, accessories and training	Completed	Oct 2001 — Nov 2005	$341,000

Name	Summary	Status	Period	Size of investment
	Healthcare			
Health sector project	The main objective of this project is to improve the health condition and equip the health center in order to enable it to provide all treatment for patients with diseases of heart, kidneys, liver and lungs. it will also attract patients from other neighboring countries	Completed	Feb 1998 – Sep 2000	$11,560,713
	Public administration			
Preparation of Preliminary Institutional Framework Study for the OIC Food Security Organization	Preparation of Preliminary Institutional Framework Study for the OIC Food Security Organization	Active	Apr 2014 – Dec 2019	$308,570
Al pari service LLP	Al pari service LLP	Completed	Nov 2008 – Apr 2011	$ 7,500,000
	Education			
23rd Meeting of the Special Program for the Economies of Central Asia (SPECA)	Construction of secondary school	Completed	Jul 2018 – Dec 2018	$22,000
Extension of the Egyptian University Culture of Islamic Culture, Almaty, Kazakhstan	The construction, furnishing and equipping of the New academic Building of the University which consists of Lecture Halls, Classrooms, Conference hall, Language & Computer laboratories and General Library with a total built_up of 6.000 sq.m, on a 6 hecta	Completed	Jan 2010 – Jan 2016	$1,000,000

Name	Summary	Status	Period	Size of investment
Additional grant for the renovation & equipping of Iqra University, Almaty, Kazakhstan	Complete the renovation works of the building	Completed	Sep 2003 — Jan 2004	$150,000
N.Nazarbaev educational foundation	N.Nazarbaev educational foundation	Completed	Aug 2003 — May 2008	$212,000
Prod.cooperative (pc) Nursultan Nazarbaev	Prod.cooperative (pc) Nursultan Nazarbaev	Completed	Jul 2002 — May 2007	$330,000
Iqra University, Almaty, Kazakhstan	To renovate building purchased for the university	Completed	Dec 2001 — Mar 2003	$250,000
One Islamic Institute and six Quranic schools	Construction/purchase of an Islamic institute and 6 Quranic schools	Completed	May 1995 — Nov 2002	$355,000
Meeting of the ministers of transport of eco in Kazakhstan	To provide conference and studies	Completed	Aug 1993 — Aug 2014	$137,000
Post Infrastructure				
Modernization of Postal Services Project	The project aims at restructuring of the mail services and postal savings system of Kazpost with a view to making it commercially oriented and competitive through introduction of new technology and effective management information system. In addition, the project will improve postal services, including postal savings services, transfer of pensions, postal orders and transportation of bank notes and	Completed	1 Sep 2003 — 29 Apr 2007	$9,000,000

Name	Summary	Status	Period	Size of investment
	money orders all over the country as well as handling mail and collecting deposits through its postal offices. The project includes provision of postal and banking equipment, training, consultancy for design and project supervision, project implementation unit, etc.			
Preparation of a Detailed Study for Modernization of Mail Services and Establishment of Postal Savings System	The TA is for (i) restructuring the postal services to make it commercially oriented and competitive by introduction of new technology; (ii) modernizing the mail services and establishing a postal saving system with effective MIS; (iii) matching and complying with the demand for modern postal services; and the increased volume of other relevant activities; (iv) enabling to be capable of offering postal savings, transfer of pensions, postal orders and transportation of bank notes and money orders all over the country in addition to handling mail and collecting deposits through its saving banks	Completed	2 Oct 2002 — 17 Aug 2003	$238,864
Energy				
SAIMAN CJSC	SAIMAN CJSC	Completed	Mar 2001 — May 2015	$ 100 000
Total			87 pcs.	$1,453,486,657

The IDB deals in Uzbekistan

Name	Summary	Status	Period	Size of investment
	Finance			
Global Line of Finance — Uzbekistan1	Global Line of Finance — Uzbekistan1 Sector: Finance (Trade (Murabaha))	Active	Dec 2019 — Jan 2020	$55,000
Uzbekistan Leasing Company (Taiba)	Uzbekistan Leasing Company (Taiba) Sector: Finance (Equity)	Active	Dec 2019 — Jan 2020	$48,930
Waqf Seminar in Uzbekistan under Islamic Finance Awareness Program	Support Islamic Finance Program	Active	Nov 2018 — Aug 2019	$3,000
QQB	QQB Sector: Finance (Trade (Murabaha))	Active	Nov 2017 — Mar 2018	$10,000,000
Uzbek GLOF	Uzbek GLOF Sector: Finance (Trade (Murabaha))	Active	Dec 2016 — Mar 2018	$70,000,000
Taiba Leasing Company	Taiba Leasing Company Sector: Finance (Trade (Murabaha))	Active	Jan 2016 — Mar 2018	$5,000,000
Equity	Equity Sector: Finance (Equity)	Active	Aug 2014 — Mar 2018	$7,000,000
Taiba Leasing Company	Taiba Leasing Company Sector: Finance (Trade (Murabaha))	Active	Jan 2014 — Mar 2018	$5,000,000
Uzbek Leasing International	Uzbek Leasing International Sector: Finance (Trade (Murabaha))	Active * 2	Jan 2014 — Mar 2018	$10,000,000
Global Line of Finance — Uzbekistan3	Global Line of Finance — Uzbekistan3 Sector: Finance (Trade (Murabaha))	Active * 2	Sep 2013 — Mar 2018	$100,000,000
World Sustainable Fund	World Sustainable Fund Sector: Finance (Equity)	Active	Dec 2012 — Mar 2018	$6,000,000

Name	Summary	Status	Period	Size of investment
Global Line of Finance — Uzbekistan2	Global Line of Finance — Uzbekistan2 Sector: Finance (Trade (Murabaha))	Active * 2	Sep 2011 — Mar 2018	$ 60 000 000
Uzbekistan Leasing Company (Taiba)	Uzbekistan Leasing Company (Taiba) Sector: Finance (Equity)	Active	Jul 2009 — Mar 2018	$5,000,000
Global Line of Finance — Uzbekistan1	Global Line of Finance — Uzbekistan1 Sector: Finance (Trade (Murabaha))	Active	Feb 2009 — Mar 2018	$50,000,000
Second Line of Financing to National Bank of Uzbekistan under Full Delegation of Authority	The second line of financing is intended to: (i) continue providing access to longer term funds, and (ii) contribute to economic growth through increased lending to SMEs. NBU will be delegated full authority to identify, select and approve projects for a bank guarantee	Completed	Jun 2008 — Dec 2015	$15,000,000
Global line of financing to three banks for SMEs	The objective of the line is to extend financing to small and medium enterprises in Uzbekistan through Asaka Bank, Ipoteka Bank and Uzpromstroybank	Completed	Jul 2007 — Dec 2011	$15,000,000
CNPS	CNPS Sector: Finance (Trade (Murabaha))	Active	Apr 2006 — Mar 2018	$1,000,000
Uzbek Leasing International	Uzbek Leasing International Sector: Finance (Trade (Murabaha))	Active	Apr 2006 — Mar 2018	$1,000,000
Ipak Yuli Bank	Ipak Yuli Bank Sector: Finance (Instalment Sale)	Active	Jan 2006- Mar 2018	$2,000,000

Name	Summary	Status	Period	Size of investment
Extension of Line of Financing to the National Bank of Uzbekistan Project	The project is to extend financing to Small and Medium Enterprises in Uzbekistan through the extension of line of financing to the National Bank of Uzbekistan. The IDB's participation will vary from project to project based on the financial requirement of each sub-project. The procurement procedures of IDB Components for subprojects will be in accordance with the IDB procurement guidelines	Completed	Sep 2004 — Jul 2011	$15,000,000
	Industry			
ADC -Asian Diamond Classic	ADC -Asian Diamond Classic Sector: Industry & Mining (Trade (Murabaha))	Active	Dec 2019 — Jan 2020	$18,000
Leading Force — II	Leading Force — II Sector: Industry & Mining (Trade (Murabaha))	Active	Feb 2019 — Jan 2020	$23,300
Aluminum System LLC	Aluminum System LLC Sector: Industry & Mining (Trade (Murabaha))	Active	Aug 2018 — Jan 2020	$35,000,000
Asian Diamond Classic — II	Asian Diamond Classic — II Sector: Industry & Mining (Trade (Murabaha))	Active	Nov 2017 — Mar 2018	$9,000,000
Aluminum System LLC	Aluminum System LLC Sector: Industry & Mining (Trade (Murabaha))	Active	May 2017 — Mar 2018	$6,000,000
JV Gold Lida	JV Gold Lida Sector: Industry & Mining (Trade (Murabaha))	Active	Aug 2014 — Mar 2018	$7,000,000
ADC-Asian Diamond Classic	ADC -Asian Diamond Classic Sector: Industry & Mining (Trade (Murabaha))	Active	Nov 2013 — Mar 2018	$9,000,000

Name	Summary	Status	Period	Size of investment
Magnus Industrial Group	Magnus Industrial Group Sector: Industry & Mining (Trade (Murabaha))	Active	Dec 2012 – Mar 2018	$6,000,000
Khausak-Shady and Kandym (KSK) Gas Field Project	The project aims to support Phase 2 of the KSK Gas Fields Development with the ultimate objective of developing and exploiting proven Gas reserves of the group of Kandym Gas fields and increasing production of fields developed in Phase 1	Completed	Mar 2012 – May 2014	$100,000,000
Leading Force – I	Leading Force – I Sector: Industry & Mining (Trade (Murabaha))	Active	Mar 2012 – Mar 2018	$2,100,000
LAZZAT MEVA	LAZZAT MEVA	Completed	Jul 2010 – Jan 2013	$1,764,015
SIRKECHI TASHTEKSTIL	SIRKECHI TASHTEKSTIL	Completed	Jun 2010 – May 2015	$1,238,694
BUTSIFAL GROUP LLC	BUTSIFAL GROUP LLC	Completed	Mar 2010 – May 2015	$475,277
SOHIL UMMON BARAKA LLC	SOHIL UMMON BARAKA LLC	Completed	Jan 2010 – Apr 2011	$399,400
PSE ABK	PSE ABK	Completed	Aug 2009 – Sep 2011	$4,794,064
TEMUR MALIK	TEMUR MALIK	Completed	Aug 2009 – Apr 2011	$1,008,990
PARABOLA LLC	PARABOLA LLC	Completed	Aug 2009 – Apr 2011	$168,427
Eco gaz system sevis LLC	Eco gaz system sevis LLC	Completed	Aug 2009 – Apr 2011	$381,000
Meyor qurilish stil LLC	Meyor qurilish stil LLC	Completed	May 2009 – Apr 2011	$881,600
POROLON LUX LLC	POROLON LUX LLC	Completed	Feb 2009 – May 2015	$450,000
POLIFLEKS	POLIFLEKS	Completed	Dec 2008 – Apr 2011	$3,350,000
UNIMAXAVTOYUL LLC	UNIMAXAVTOYUL LLC	Active	Nov 2008 – Jan 2020	$140,380

Name	Summary	Status	Period	Size of investment
AVANGARD PROM STORY	AVANGARD PROM STORY	Completed	Oct 2008 — Jan 2013	$862,550
Yaypan Ishonch Mebel	Yaypan Ishonch Mebel	Completed	Sep 2008 — Apr 2011	$397,000
NATIONAL PLAST	NATIONAL PLAST	Completed	Jul 2008 — Oct 2012	$2,002,260
STELLARIS PROJECT	STELLARIS PROJECT	Completed	Jul 2008 — Apr 2011	$526,408
MEBEL DILVAZIZ	MEBEL DILVAZIZ	Completed	Apr 2008 — May 2015	$150,000
Purchasing of Two Airplanes for Uzbekistan Airways Project	The project aims at purchasing two airplanes in order to enhance economic efficiency, competitiveness, flight safety as well as opportunity o further increase the level of passenger carrying capacity of Uzbekistan Airways.	Completed	May 2013 — Dec 2013	$168,102,253
URG-GAZ-KARPET (PHASE II)	URG-GAZ-KARPET (PHASE II)	Completed	Mar 2008 — Apr 2011	$4,973,644
BAHT-R	BAHT-R	Completed	Feb 2008 — Apr 2011	$544,120
HYDROLIFE BOTTLERS	HYDROLIFE BOTTLERS	Completed	Dec 2007 — Apr 2011	$2,561,985
DOVON agro!	DOVON	Completed	Dec 2007 — Dec 2012	$490,200
The joint stock co. «Humo-Uch»	The joint stock co. «Humo-Uch»	Completed	Mar 2006 — Mar 2008	$3,621,300
JSC»Rishton-Teks»	The joint-stock co. «Rishton-Teks»	Completed	Mar 2006 — Mar 2008	$4,700,000
JSC»Urg-Gaz-Karpet»	The joint venture «Urg-Gaz-Karpet»	Completed	Feb 2006- Jun 2008	$787,771
FARM SEMRUG	FARM SEMRUG	Completed	Jul 2005 — Jul 2009	$133,975
Modernization & Expansion Project in OJSC	Modernization & Expansion Project in OJSC Sector: Finance (Leasing)	Active	Feb 2005 — Mar 2018	$4,000,000

Name	Summary	Status	Period	Size of investment
Yadem Tekstil Company — Sukuk Financing	The Sukuk_based funding for the project is to be through two operations: (i) The Purchase and Leaseback of part of Yadem's existing plant equipment, which was inspected and identified by the due diligence mission during the visit to Yadem's manufacturing facilities; and (ii) Direct Lease financing for the purchase and installation of a new Spinning Mill.	Completed	Sep 2004 — Dec 2008	$23,091,220
Textile	Textile Sector: Finance (Leasing)	Completed	Feb 2004 — Mar 2018	$750,000
Spinning equip.Joint Venture Alisher Navoi Intl.	Spinning equip.Joint Venture Alisher Navoi Intl. Sector: Finance (Leasing)	Completed	Feb 2004 — Mar 2018	$6,850,000
Healthcare				
VitaMed Medical Center	VitaMed Medical Center Sector: Health (Trade (Murabaha))	Active	Jun 2019 — Jan 2020	$145,000
ATM Group	ATM Group Sector: Health (Trade (Murabaha))	Active	May 2017 — Mar 2018	$10,000,000
Jurabek Laboratories III	Jurabek Laboratories III Sector: Health (Trade (Murabaha))	Active	Feb 2017 — Mar 2018	$10,000,000
The Support to Upgrading of Public Health Laboratories Project	The project aims at contributing to the efforts of Uzbekistan to ensure safe public health services through prevention and control of major communicable and environmental related diseases. The project will improve the capacity and quality of the existing Public Health Laboratories throughout the country. This objective will be achieved through rehabilitation of target 158 PHLs and provision of modern equipment	Active	Jun 2014 — Jan 2020	$17,440,000

Name	Summary	Status	Period	Size of investment
Jurabek Laboratories II	Jurabek Laboratories II Sector: Health (Trade (Murabaha))	Active * 2	Jan 2014 – Mar 2018	$10,000,000
Support to Development of Oncology Services Project	The project aims at improving access to and the quality of medical diagnostics and treatment services for cancer patients through the establishment of Oncology Centers and provision of modern medical equipment at different locations in Uzbekistan that will offer high standard of medical services. This will be achieved through construction of 2 new centers and rehabilitating of 13 existing ones, in addition to acquisition of medical equipment and training of health care providers. The project will benefit about 134,000 cancer patients across the country	Active	Apr 2012 – Jan 2020	$37,040,000
State Medical Emergency Hospitals Equipment Project	The project aims at enhancing the developmental efforts of the Government in maintaining appropriate health standards of the population through the provision of modern medical equipment to 12 Emergency Medical Hospitals at different locations in Uzbekistan to enable them to provide emergency and necessary medical services. The project scope includes: Civil works; Emergency Medical Equipment including training spare/parts; Consultancy Services; etc.	Completed	Apr 2004 – Sep 2010	$23,799,000
Medical equipment for science center for surgery, formerly hospital	Reallocated to purchase of medical equipment (Ultra sound device) on 20/9/99	Completed	May 1992 – Aug 2014	$250,000

Name	Summary	Status	Period	Size of investment
	Housing construction			
Construction of Modern Rural Housing Project (Phase-2) 2017	The Project aims to expand access to affordable and improved housing, equipped with associated basic infrastructure as well as social and market facilities, for the rural population in 6 regions of Uzbekistan	Active	Apr 2017 — Aug 2019	$113,000,000
Construction of Modern Rural Housing Project (Phase-2) 2018	The Project aims to expand access to affordable and improved housing, equipped with associated basic infrastructure as well as social and market facilities, for the rural population in 6 regions of Uzbekistan	Active	Apr 2017 — Jan 2020	$93,000,000
Construction of Modern Rural Housing Project (Phase-2) 2019	The Project aims to expand access to affordable and improved housing, equipped with associated basic infrastructure as well as social and market facilities, for the rural population in 6 regions of Uzbekistan	Active	Apr 2017 — Jan 2020	$94,000,000
Construction of Modern Rural Housing Project (Phase-I)	The Project aims to expand access to affordable and improved housing, equipped with associated basic infrastructure as well as social and market facilities, for the rural population. This is expected to contribute to the overall goal of the HIRDS, to improve the living standards in rural areas. Upon completion, the key expected results include (i) new, modern and affordable houses to 1,100 rural families, (ii) improved engineering infrastructure networks in 23 rural settlements, and (iii) improved services through access to social and market related facilities to approximately 4,500 people	Completed	Oct 2014 — Mar 2017	$100,000,000

Name	Summary	Status	Period	Size of investment
	Education and science			
Promotion of Employment of Rural Women through Implementation of Socially Inclusive Business Projects	To expand rural women's access to sustainable income in rural Uzbekistan by implementing socially inclusive business projects in 13 regions	Active	Aug 2018 — Dec 2019	$100,000
Support to the Development of Higher Education Project	The project aims at contributing to improve the learning environment and quality of higher education of the existing institutions. By 2020 the project will benefit about 25,000 students and 156 lecturers/staff. The project includes (i) construction of 6 new academic buildings with a total space of 13,244 m^2, and related infrastructure, (ii) renovating 6 existing academic buildings, (iii) procuring laboratory furniture and equipment; (iv) providing training for academic staff; (v) organizing study visits, (vi) research and development; (vii) curricula development; (viii) supporting project management	Active	May 2017 — Jan 2020	$44,480,000
Support to Secondary Education Sector	The project aims at contributing to the alleviation of rural poverty in Uzbekistan through providing 2,800 secondary school students in poor rural areas with quality education and appropriate knowledge that will prepare them for vocational and technical education and enter the job market with relevant skills. This will be achieved through constructing and equipping 13 secondary schools, each having enrolment capacity of 216 students, in the rural areas in 8 regions of Uzbekistan	Completed	Nov 2010 — Jan 2017	$12,202,218

Name	Summary	Status	Period	Size of investment
Construction and Equipping of Vocational Colleges Project	The project aims at enhancing the developmental efforts of the Government in providing appropriate higher education standards for the population, in order to mitigate the shortage of skilled manpower by improving access to quality vocational education, and to mitigate the present geographical imbalance in the distribution of vocational education facilities. The project will include construction and equipping of five new vocational colleges at different locations. This will provide education to 2,700 students annually	Completed	May 2007 — Apr 2015	$10,846,244
Construction and equipping of secondary schools	The main objective is to facilitate government initiative to improve the socio-economic standards in the rural areas through the construction of 13 new secondary schools which will have among other benefits an immediate tangible effect of providing quality modern educational facilities to 4,135 students	Completed	May 2006 — Feb 2010	$9,957,500
Additional grant for participation in equipping and furnishing of Imam Al-Bukahry	To complete the furnishing and equipping of Imam Al_Bukahry Institute (Madrassa Dar Al Hadith)	Completed	Sep 2003 — May 2007	$100,000
Printing press for Tashkent Islamic University	Setting up of printing press	Completed	Jul 2001 — May 2005	$395,000
Rehab. of Kokaldash Islamic inst in Tashkent, formerly (constr. of 8 Quranic schools)	Construction of Islamic Institute, etc	Completed	May 1992 — Aug 2014	$200,000

Name	Summary	Status	Period	Size of investment
Isl sch & hostel in Samarkand (Darul Hadith Madrasa/ Imam Al Bukhari complex)	Construction of schools and hostel	Completed	May 1992 — Aug 2014	$230,000
Construction of hostel for Mir Arab Islamic Institute in Boukhara	Construction of hostel and other facilities	Active	May 1991 — Jan 2020	$295,516
Preparation of a Development Study for the International Innovation Centre for the Aral Sea Basin	To support the establishment of an international center of excellence for research, innovation and development in saline environments through leadership and partnership for sustainable livelihoods and ecosystems of the Aral Sea region	Active	Apr 2019 — Jan 2020	$278,158
Preparing a Sustainability Study and Purchase of Scanning and Digitization Equipment for the Imam Al Bukhari International Scientific Research Centre	Identification of the financial sustainability of Imam Al Bukhari International Scientific Research Center and the purchase of scanning and digitalization equipment and training	Active	Sep 2018 — Jan 2020	$279,996
	Road construction			
Reconstruction and Upgrading of M39 Road in Surkhandarya Region	The project aims at improving transport efficiency and promoting economic development in Uzbekistan through the reconstruction and upgrading of a portion of about 100 km of the M39 road "Almaty-Bishkek-Tashkent-Termez" in Surkhandarya Region. As a result, transport cost and travel time on the proposed road will be reduced and safety improved	Active	Nov 2010 — Jan 2020	$167,200,000

Name	Summary	Status	Period	Size of investment
Road Construction and Maintenance Equipment Project	The project is to facilitate the construction, regular maintenance and upkeep of municipal roads of Tashkent City by providing modem road construction and maintenance equipment and through the upgrading of existing Asphalt Plant. The project will help to set up a preventive and corrective maintenance program for the road network in and around Tashkent thus reducing the need for major rehabilitation and reconstruction of roads in the future	Completed	Sep 2004 – Feb 2011	$12,557,000
Water supply and irrigation				
Reconstruction and expansion of sewerage systems of in the three cities of Gulistan, Shirin, and Yangier of Syrdarya region	The project aims to improve the coverage and quality of the sanitation services in the three cities of Gulistan, Shirin, and Yangiyer in the Syrdarya Region of Uzbekistan. The project will benefit approximately 140,000 residents of the cities through reconstruction and development of the wastewater treatment facilities, and expansion of the sanitation networks and pumping stations	Active	Dec 2016 – Jan 2020	$57,500,000
Improvement of Water Resources Management of Hazarbag Irrigation in Surkhandarya Region Project	The project aims at contributing to food security by improving agricultural production and productivity. At completion, the project will have (i) increased the yields of main crops by 37%, (ii) increased the production of wheat, vegetables and fruits by441,769 tons per year, (iii) increased farmers' income by $3,644 per year, (v) increased water flow from 50 m3/sec to 110 m3/sec, (vi) increased canals efficiency from 55% to 75%, (vii) reduced O&M and Energy cost of the irrigation system by $7 mln/year	Active	Jun 2014 – Jan 2020	$89,550,000

142

Name	Summary	Status	Period	Size of investment
Reconstruction of Main Irrigation Canals of Tashsaka Irrigation System	The project aims at contributing to food security and helping enhance agricultural income through improved agricultural production and productivity by reconstruction of irrigation canals that will enhance water availability. The project will increase the agricultural production by 181,690 tons and will create 90,000 jobs for farm workers as well as increasing net income per farmer by $ 3,602/year	Active	Nov 2012 – Jan 2020	$90,370,000
Tashkent Sewerage Project	The project aims at improving the environmental conditions, as well as the reliability, efficiency and sustainability of wastewater management in Tashkent City through (i) Rehabilitation of wastewater treatment infrastructure, (ii) Limited expansion of the sewerage network, (iii) Provision of wastewater quality monitoring equipment, and (iv) acquisition of infrastructure maintenance equipment	Completed	May 2020 – Jul 2017	$35,370,000
Reconstruction of Irrigation and Drainage Networks in Djizzakh and Syrdaria Regions	The project aims at increasing agricultural productivity mainly of cotton, cereals, fruits and vegetables, thus contributing to food security and increasing per capita income and living standards of the target population. This will be achieved through (i) Reconstruction, Extension and Improvement of the existing irrigation and drainage systems, and (ii) Improving the agricultural support services for the lower income groups, as well as supporting the institutional/capacity of the Water Users Associations	Completed	Jun 2009 – Dec 2013	$52,649,000

Name	Summary	Status	Period	Size of investment
	Energy			
500 kV Guzar-Surkhan transmission line substations	The main objective is to strengthen the existing electricity transmission infrastructure in the South of Uzbekistan thus meeting the demand within Uzbek border as well as for future export of surplus power to Afghanistan	Completed	Sep 2008 — Dec 2011	$37,994,921
Efficient Outdoor Lighting for Tashkent City Project	The project aims at enhancing energy efficiency and provide reliable and efficient electricity for outdoor lighting by helping modernize the power generation systems. This will help conserve natural gas which is a precious energy resource and an important means of foreign exchange earning for the Country. Modernizing and enhancing energy efficiency of the outdoor lighting system of the Tashkent city	Active	Apr 2013 — Aug 2019	$36,000,000
500 kV Syrdarya to Sogdiana Transmission Line Project	The project aims at ensuring a reliable and efficient transmission of electricity from Syrdarya power station to Sogdiana substation so as to cover the growing deficit of power in Samarkand _ Bukhara region, which has a population of over 4 mln. Completion of the project would lead to economic growth and help in meeting the growing demand of electricity for the domestic, commercial and industrial consumers in these areas. The transmission line will meet the demand gap and strengthen the 500 kV grid system. The project will include 500 kV Single Circuit Transmission Line, Substation Extensions, Construction, Erection and Commissioning; Consultancy services; etc.	Completed	Sep 2004 — Apr 2011	$ 25,08, 000

Name	Summary	Status	Period	Size of investment
	Public administration			
T.A. Grant for UZINFOINVEST	The project aims to enhance Uzbekistan's capacity to attract foreign direct investment by enabling UZINFOINVEST to promote opportunities for investment through marketing; promotion materials and training of staff of UzinfoInvest in developing investment promotion strategies	Completed	May 2012 – Aug 2016	$300,000
C.B. of the Chamber of Commerce and Industry	The objective is to enable Chamber of Commerce and Industry of Uzbekistan to disseminate information and consulting services to the local entrepreneurs in all regions of the country	Completed	Aug 2007 – Apr 2012	$150,000
C.B. of the Ministry of Finance	The objective of the project is to facilitate establishment of the training center under the fiscal policy center of the Ministry of Finance	Completed	May 2005 – May 2011	$277,970
F.S. for investment holding company	The main objective is to evaluate whether the proposed investment holding company is well founded and is likely to fulfill the main goals and objectives set by IDB and the participants of the investment conference (held in Tashkent 28/9 to 1/10/2003). The study shall evaluate the operational, economical, financial, legal, institutional managerial aspects	Completed	Sep 2004 – May 2011	$143,000
Organization of International Investment Conference in Tajikistan and Uzbekistan	The T.A. will strengthen economic ties and transfer of human and monetary capital between OIC and CIS countries. The T.A. will provide the opportunity for OIC businessmen to network and establish business relations with their counterparts in Tajikistan and Uzbekistan. It will cover air travel cost; hotel accommodations and logistics; conference and audiovisual facilities; and other related expenditures	Completed	Mar 2003 – Apr 2006	$232,000
Total		103 pcs.		*$1,990,255,286*

The IDB deals in Azerbaijan

Name	Summary	Status	Period	Size of investment
Real Estate				
Baki Plaza	Baki Plaza Sector: Real Estate (Instalment Sale)	Active	Aug 2019 — Jan 2020	$23,000
Baki Plaza	Baki Plaza Sector: Real Estate (Instalment Sale)	Active	Mar 2008 — Mar 2018	$20,000,000
Finance				
Bank Standard	Bank Standard Sector: Finance (Instalment Sale)	Active	Oct 2019 — Nov 2019	$23,500
International Bank of Azerbaijan	International Bank of Azerbaijan Sector: Finance (Trade (Murabaha))	Active	Jul 2019 — Jan 2020	$10,000
International Bank of Azerbaijan	International Bank of Azerbaijan Sector: Finance (Trade (Murabaha))	Active	Jul 2013 — Mar 2018	$20,000
Development of Legal Framework for Islamic Finance in Azerbaijan	T.A. aims at recruiting consultants for assisting the Azerbaijan in developing a suitable legal framework for Islamic Finance. This will involve review of the existing legal framework in the context of banking activities in Azerbaijan. It will propose a legal framework for Islamic Finance i.e. Amendments in Law on Banks or draft a separate Islamic banking law and amendments in law on Central Bank of Azerbaijan and other laws as needed	Active	Jan 2017 — Jan 2020	$200,000
Unibank (2)	Unibank (2) Sector: Finance (Trade (Murabaha))	Active	Nov 2014 — Jan 2018	$10,000,000
Unibank (2)	Unibank (2) Sector: Finance (Trade (Murabaha))	Active	Nov 2014 — Jan 2018	$10,000,000
Global Line of Finance Azerbaijan	Global Line of Finance Azerbaijan Sector: Finance (Trade (Murabaha))	Active	Nov 2010 — Mar 2018	$40,000,000

Name	Summary	Status	Period	Size of investment
Caspian International Investment Company	Caspian International Investment Company Sector: Finance (Equity)	Active	Nov 2006 — Mar 2018	$7,000,000
Bank Standard	Bank Standard Sector: Finance (Instalment Sale)	Active	Nov 2006 — Mar 2018	$3,000,000
Rabita Bank (2nd Line)	Rabita Bank ((2nd Line) Sector: Finance (Instalment Sale)	Active	Nov 2006 — Mar 2018	$1,000,000
Azerdemiryol Bank	Azerdemiryol Bank Sector: Finance (Instalment Sale)	Active	Nov 2006 — Mar 2018	$3,000,000
Turan Bank	Turan Bank Sector: Finance (Instalment Sale)	Active	Nov 2006 — Mar 2018	$1,000,000
International Bank Azerbaijan (2nd Line)	Internationa Bank Azerbaijan (2nd Line) Sector: Finance (Instalment Sale)	Active	Nov 2006 — Mar 2018	$2,000,000
UniBank	UniBank Sector: Finance (Instalment Sale)	Active	Dec 2003 — Mar 2018	$1,700,000
Internationa Bank Azerbaijan	Internationa Bank Azerbaijan (1st Line) Sector: Finance (Instalment Sale)	Active	Dec 2003 — Mar 2018	$4,500,000
Rabita Bank	Rabita Bank (1st Line) Sector: Finance (Instalment Sale)	Active	Dec 2003 — Mar 2018	$1,600,000
Azerbaijan Leasing Company (Ansar)	Azerbaijan Leasing Company (Ansar) Sector: Finance (Equity)	Active	Aug 2008 — Mar 2018	$6,200,000
C.B. of the state committee for securities	The project aims at strengthening Azerbaijan's securities market in Azerbaijan	Completed	Feb 2008 — Sep 2009	$261,900
Industry				
Home Appliances, Electrical and Electronic	Home Appliances, Electrical and Electronic Sector: Information & Communications (Trade (Murabaha))	Completed	Dec 2013 — Mar 2018	$5,000,000

Name	Summary	Status	Period	Size of investment
Home Appliances, Electrical and Electronic	Home Appliances, Electrical and Electronic Sector: Information & Communications (Trade (Murabaha))	Completed	Dec 2012 – Mar 2018	$2,000,000
Home Appliances, Electrical and Electronic	Home Appliances, Electrical and Electronic Sector: Information & Communications (Trade (Murabaha))	Completed	Dec 2011 – Nov 2018	$1,500,000
Cement Mixer	Cement Mixer Sector: Industry & Mining (Trade (Murabaha))	Completed	Aug 2011 – Mar 2018	$1,000,000
Toys, Electronic items	Toys, Electronic items Sector: Information & Communications (Trade (Murabaha))	Completed	Aug 2011 – Mar 2018	$1,500,000
Crawler Excavator, Dozers	Crawler Excavator, Dozers Sector: Industry & Mining (Trade (Murabaha))	Completed	Apr 2011 – Mar 2018	$3,500,000
Home Appliances	Home Appliances Sector: Industry & Mining (Trade (Murabaha))	Completed	Nov 2010 – Mar 2018	$1,200,000
Cement Mixer	Cement Mixer Sector: Industry & Mining (Trade (Murabaha))	Completed	Nov 2010 – Mar 2018	$3,000,000
Spare Parts of Control Valves for Control Plants	Spare Parts of Control Valves for Control Plants Sector: Industry & Mining (Trade (Murabaha))	Completed	Jun 2010 – Mar 2018	$30,000,000
Plastic and raw material	Plastic and raw material Sector: Industry & Mining (Trade (Murabaha))	Completed	May 2009 – Mar 2018	$1,000,000
Telecom.Cable Expansion proj. fvr. Hesfibel	Telecom.Cable Expansion proj. fvr. Hesfibel Sector: Finance (Leasing)	Active	Mar 2003 – Mar 2018	$10,000,000
Pharmaceutical products	Pharmaceutical products Sector: Industry & Mining (Trade (Murabaha))	Completed	Jan 2009 – Mar 2018	$1,000,000

Name	Summary	Status	Period	Size of investment
T.A. for lankaren tomato paste plant	Market survey and investigating the potentials of existing facilities preliminary design and feasibility study detailed designs and tender documents	Completed	May 1994 — Jul 2006	$132,058
Education				
Empowerment of Women Entrepreneurs Through Development of Planning Skills	The T.A. operation aims at creating better access to financial services for women through educating them on life planning, budgeting and business planning which will enable them to become economically active citizens. The operation will educate current and potential female microfinance clients with the tools necessary to strengthen women's ability to identify and overcome the barriers that prevent them from leading more satisfactory life	Completed	Oct 2013 — Aug 2016	$45,000
Construction of 5 Quranic Schools, Azerbaijan	Construction of Quranic Schools	Completed	Jun 1992	$125,000
Maahad Al Imam Al Bukhari, Baku, Azerbaijan	Construction of Al Imam Al Bukhari Institute	Completed	May 1991 — Jun 1992	$335,000
Water supply and sewerage				
Support to the National Water Supply and Sanitation Program in 6 Regions Project	The project aims at constructing new water and wastewater treatment plants and installation of new water distribution networks and sewerage collection systems. This will provide clean and safe drinking water and sewerage connections to 320,267 inhabitants (including refugees and internally displaced people) in the 6 regions	Active	Apr 2012 — Jan 2020	$200,050,000

149

Name	Summary	Status	Period	Size of investment
Reconstruction of the Mil Garabagh water collector	The main objective of the T.A. for preparing a feasibility study for the reconstruction of the Mil Garabagh water collector project	Completed	Apr 2009 – Apr 2012	$314,066
Flood Protection, Modernization and Expansion of the Irrigated Areas Project in Nakhchivan Autonomous Republic	The project aims at enhancing food security, reducing poverty and improving management of water resources and protecting lands. The project will increase water resources for irrigation, lower consumption per hectare through improved efficient water conveyance, increase irrigated land, increase agriculture production, decrease flood damages and erosion	Completed	Nov 2011 – Jan 2017	$64,830,000
Integrated Rural Development Project (Jed Declaration)	The overall goal of the IRDP is to reduce rural poverty in Agdash, Yevlakh, Sheki and Oghuz through increased food security and enhanced income-raising opportunities. The project objectives is to assist small farmers to learn how to utilize their resources effectively and efficiently to achieve better productivity and profitability and environmental sustainability from both irrigated and rained crop production and livestock keeping through delivery of effective advisory and financial services	Active	Jun 2011 – Jan 2020	$ 66,390,000
Mingechaur Hydro Power (Phase II) Project	The project aims at replacing of turbines, generators, substations and control room equipment of the existing Mingechaur Hydro Power Project in order to increase reliability on electricity supply. The project also includes reconstruction of an existing 16.5 MW Varvara Power station, a downstream power station. The project will contribute an incremental power generation capacity of 100 MW and annual energy sales of 415 GWh	Completed	Sep 2007 – Mar 2015	$80,000,000

Name	Summary	Status	Period	Size of investment
Khanarc canal (Phase II)	The project aims to irrigate existing 31114 ha an addition al of 12569 ha land to use the available water resources within the project area to the maximum extent	Completed	Nov 2001 — Jul 2008	$8,820,000
Khanrc canal project	The project envisages construction of a new water canal of 65.8 km	Completed	Dec 1998 — Feb 2006	$9,469,600
Main Mill-Mughan drainage canal project	The main objective of the project is to drain a net area of 300,000 ha of agricultural land from saline and mineralized groundwater by construction of the main Mill-Mugan collector canal. this would be realized by excavation of a 140.9 km long main collector canal excavation of 45 km long branch collector canals and construction of hydraulic structures. these efforts will result in higher agricultural production	Completed	Sep 1994 — Jan 2001	$9,854,598
F.S. of Samur Apsheron canal	Preparation of F.S. and conceptual design of expansion of Samur Apsheron irrigation canal	Completed	Feb 1993 — Jul 2006	$280,000
Samur Absheron Irrigation Project (Velvelichay-Takhtakorpu Canal)	The project aims at contributing to poverty alleviation by improving the availability of water for the development of irrigation and water supply to rural and urban population. This will be achieved through construction of the Velvelichay-Takhtakorpu Canal, which is part of the large scale Samur-Absheron Irrigation and Water Supply System	Completed	Mar 2005 — Mar 2011	$10,245900
Agriculture				
Wheat	Wheat Sector: Finance (Trade (Murabaha))	Completed	Nov 2010 — Mar 2018	$1,300,000
Integrated rural developement project	The project aims to a)facilitate the repatriation of people that have been internally displaced b)improve their standard of living through basic education, water supply, health, irrigation, roads etc.	Completed	Jul 1999 — Aug 2005	$9,734,200

151

Name	Summary	Status	Period	Size of investment
Procurement of food, medicine and agricultural equipment	Procurement of food, medicine and agricultural equipment	Completed	Nov 1992 – Feb 1999	$1,500,000
Road construction				
F.S. on Upgrading and Reconstruction of Ujar-Zardab-Agjabadi Road Project	Ujar-Zardab-Agjabedi Road helps in regional connectivity and freight transport. The study will encompass (i) Assessment of optimal allocation of resources and investment, (ii) improve regional connectivity and freight transport, and (iii) recommend the required improvement of the road based on engineering and economic analysis	Completed	Nov 2011 – Dec 2013	$303,108
Construction of Yevlakh-Ganja Road Project	The project is to improve the quality of transport on the Yevlakh-Ganja road by reducing the vehicle operating cost, and travel time. The project will improve the efficiency of the road, reduce the operating cost to vehicle owners and reduce future maintenance costs, and contribute to increased road safety for road users through reducing the frequency and severity of road accidents. The main components of the project are (i) Civil Works, (ii) Construction Supervision, (iii) Project Management Unit and (iv) Financial Auditing	Completed	Mar 2005 – Jan 2012	$10,104,910
Reconstruction of Ujar-Yevlakh Road Project	The project aims at reconstruction of the severely deteriorated existing 40 years old single carriageway Ujar-Yevlakh road and installation of the required safety devices to improve the quality of transport on the road by reducing vehicle operating cost, travel time, accidents and negative environmental impacts (vehicle emissions). The reconstruction of the road will also facilitate the transport of agricultural and industrial products	Completed	May 2004 – May 2010	$22,000,000

Name	Summary	Status	Period	Size of investment
Alyat Ghazi Mohamed road	The project aims to upgrade the existing Alyat Gazi Mohamed road 2 lane undivided with 3.75m lane width which is approximately 44 km along to a dual 4 lane divided asphalt carriage way highway	Completed	Jun 2007 — Jun 2015	$13,822,886
Detailed eng. design tender doc.for road (Gazi-Mohd) city	Engineering design and preparation of tender documents for the construction of Gazi Alyat Mohammed road	Completed	Jul 1992 — Jul 2006	$238,695
Waste processing infrustructure				
Baku waste to energy plant	The main objective of the project is to improve the ecologic al and health conditions in the Greater Baku area, including the capital city Baku, by constructing the first Waste to Energy plant capable of treating 500000 tons of waste per year	Completed	Jun 2010 — Jul 2012	$197,590,635
Energy				
Janub power plant	The main objective of the project is to provide reliable power supply increase the efficiency of the power generation system in Azerbaijan through the construction of a state of the art 780 MW Gas fired combined cycle Janub power plant	Completed	Dec 2009 — Jun 2013	$191,075,682
Khachmaz Electric Substations and Transmission Line Project	The project is to provide quality and reliable power supply to Northeastern region of Azerbaijan at the lowest financial cost. This will be realized through the construction of 330/110 kV substation connected at 330 kV side and construction of 24 km 110 kV TL which will connect this substation with 110 kV distribution network. This will accelerate economic growth and meet the growing demand of electricity for the domestic, commercial and industrial consumers in northern part of AZ	Completed	Jun 2005 — Apr 2011	$13,508,000

Name	Summary	Status	Period	Size of investment
Prep. of tender docs. tender eval. for the Mingechaur power	The project aims at preparation of tender documents for IDB components of Mingechaur power project which enable Azerenergy to implement the project quickly	Completed	Mar 1999 — Sep 2003	$200,000
Mingechaur power project	The project aims at retiring old and inefficient power stations which would result in energy saving and improving supply of electricity	Completed	Nov 1998 — Sep 2003	$12,520,000
Public administration				
Strengthen the debt management capacity of the cabinet of ministers	The objective of the project is to strengthen the debt management capacity of the cabinet of ministers of Azerbaijan through establishing the central monitoring system within its external borrowings department	Completed	Oct 2008 — Feb 2013	$322,350
IDB int'l investment conference in Azerbaijan	T.A. aims at strengthening economic ties and trade cooperation and investment between OIC member countries and Azerbaijan	Completed	Aug 2006 — Jul 2007	$255,988
Strengthening the Capacity of the Ministry of Economic Development Project	The T.A. is to improve the institutional capacity of the Ministry of Economic Development. In particular, the project will assist in strengthening the institutional capacity of the Secretariat for the State Rural Development Program and its Regional Units to coordinate the implementation of the State Program on Socio-Economic Development of Regions	Completed	May 2006 — Sep 2011	$265,737
C.B. for ministry of finance	It is to improve the revenue collection management of fiscal expenditures of the government of Azerbaijan	Completed	Dec 2001 — Feb 2006	$361,800
Emergency assistance to victims and forced migrants				
Improvement of Physical and Social	On 25 Nov 2000 an earthquake struck Azerbaijan 85 km to the North-East of Baku. It caused 26 deaths,	Completed	Apr 2003 — Jun 2007	$8,939,000

Name	Summary	Status	Period	Size of investment
Infrastructure Facilities Affected by the Earthquake of Nov 2000	rendered over 141,000 people homeless and damaged infrastructure, industry, and private property of about 7,796 sites costing around US$ 41.60 mln. The project aims at mitigating the effects of the earthquake by restoring the damaged facilities			
Construction of Social Infrastructure Facilities Project for IDPs	The project aims at improving the living standards of IDPs through contributing to the construction of the education and health facilities as well as a drinking water supply system for the new settlements being constructed by Government in Bilesuvar and Fizuli regions. Education infrastructure for all schooling levels will be provided through construction of 14 schools and provision of basic furniture and laboratory equipment. Health system will be established through constructing 14 medical units for the new settlements and provision of modem medical equipment which will facilitate quality diagnosis of health condition of the IDPs. The drinking water supply system will comprise boring of wells, water conveyance, storage and distribution network	Completed	Dec 2005 — Sep 2009	$10,292,100
Airport infrastructure				
New hanger at Baku int'l airport (first phase)	To conduct a study to determine the techno-economic feasibility of constructing a new hangar at Baku international airport to meet aircraft services maintenance requirements of Azerbaijan airlines and neighboring Central Asian republics the study will also include preliminary design of the hangar supporting facilities and equipment	Completed	Feb 1993 — Jul 2006	$254,228
Total		66 pcs.		*$1,117,718,941*

The IDB deals in Turkmenistan

Name	Summary	Status	Period	Size of investment
	Telecommunication			
Telecommunication Network Enhancement Project	The objective is to contribute to the economic growth of the country through developing the Turkmenistan telecommunication system. It includes installing technologies enablers into the network operators to offer users a wider range of more advanced services while achieving greater network capacity through improved spectral efficiency	Active	Nov 2017 — Jan 2020	$273,000,000
Telecommunication Infrastructure Project	The project aims at developing the telecommunication infrastructure in Turkmenistan through the interconnection of 9 cities to the telephone and data networks using optical fiber cable and by increasing the capacity of telephone digital exchanges in the capital Ashgabat. It also aims at improving international access through linkage with the Global Telecom. Network. Most of the telecommunication equipment and systems date back to the 60s and are in need of major refurbishment. a fiber optic communication cable will connect Ashgabat with Turkmenbashy and pass through Bakherden– Serdar–Bereket Balkanabat, for a total length of 608 km along with all associated hardware and software to be installed in the 9 stations. Additional capacity of 15,000 new telephone lines will be created through adding new remote stations and expanding the capacities of existing ones. a long term consultant will assist the executing agency in preparing the technical specifications, evaluation of bids and for project supervision	Completed	Oct 2001 — Jan 2008	$15,118,000

Name	Summary	Status	Period	Size of investment
	Oil and gas transportation			
TAPI Gas Pipeline Project (including Phase-1 of $350 mln for 2016 and Phase-2 of $ 350 mln for 2017)	The project aims at enhancing the sub-regional economic cooperation among Turkmenistan, Afghanistan, Pakistan and India based on the needs of the market economy through expanding the use of natural gas resources. The TAPI gas pipeline project will help in exporting up to 33 (bcm) of natural gas per year, approximately 1800 kilometer (km) long, from Turkmenistan to Afghanistan, Pakistan, and India	Active	Oct 2016 — Jan 2020	$700,000,000
Procurement of two new oil tankers	The main objective of the project is to enhance the country' s capacity in exporting its energy resources to regional international markets	Completed	Jun 2009 — Apr 2011	$31,000,000
New oil tanker	To procure a new oil tanker of 5,000 dwt capacity to operate in the Caspian sea which will expand the existing fleet of 4 ships of Turkmen shipping company to meet the growing demand to export crude oil and petroleum products to neighbouring countries	Completed	Jun 1997 — Sep 2002	$11,000,000
	Railroad infrastructure			
Construction of Bereket-Etrek Railway Project (Tranche 1)	The project is a part of the main project of 936 km long North–South railway corridor linking Kazakhstan, Turkmenistan and Iran. Railway tracks of 724 km long will be constructed inside Turkmenistan. The Northern section of 467 km long railway track is being constructed by the Government from its own sources. The remaining section (Southern) of 257 km railway tracks with 69 km auxiliary lines will jointly be covered by IDB financing and the Government	Completed	Jan 2010 — Feb 2016	$190,900,000

Name	Summary	Status	Period	Size of investment
Construction of Bereket-Etrek Railway Project (Tranche 2)	–	Active	Jan 2010 – Jun 2019	$197,146,554
Energy				
F.S. of silicon production from Karakum sand	The objective of the project is to assess the feasibility of using the Karakum desert sand in Turkmenistan for commercial production of solar grade silicon to be used for the manufacturing of solar cells	Completed	Jun 2009 – May 2012	$189,684
Road construction				
F.S. and Preliminary Design of Turkmenbashy-Karabogaz Road Project	The T.A. is to assist the Government in preparing a Feasibility Study and Preliminary Design of a project suitable for financing to connect the city of Turkmenbashy, which is a major gateway for Turkmenistan trade with Europe to the international road network of Kazakhstan and other neighbouring countries. The project will aim to reconstruct and rehabilitate selected sections of the Turkmenbashy-Kazakh border road section (225 km)	Completed	Aug 2004 – Feb 2008	$275,000
Healthcare				
Archman medical hydrotherapy center	To expand usage of medical hydro therapy for the treatment of chronic internal diseases. It will also strengthen the preventive health care system that is an part of the socio-economic development program	Completed	May2005 – Mar 2012	$9,108,073

Name	Summary	Status	Period	Size of investment
Mary Diagnostics Center Project	The project aims at strengthening the diagnostic capability of the medical system and improvement in the delivery of quality healthcare at velayat (province) level. The project is part of a program under which 3 diagnostics centers are to be established in 3 velayats (provinces) to strengthen and support the local health care system. The project will include: Civil Works, Procurement of Medical Equipment, furniture, etc.	Completed	Oct 2002 – May 2006	$5,500,000
Diagnostic centers project	The main objective of the project is to strengthen the diagnostic capability of the medical system and to continue the improvement of the delivery of quality health care at Velayat(district) level. The project will establish two diagnostic centers, one in Ashgabot and other at Doshoguz. Each one will provide medical equipment	Completed	May 2000 – Oct2005	$10,330,368
Turkmenbashi referral and training hospital	To equip the already constructed Turkmenbashi referral and training hospital with modern medical equipment and facilities for providing diagnosis, treatment as well as clinical training for internees, resident doctors, nurses and paramedical professionals	Completed	May 1996 – Dec 1997	$5,250,000
	Education			
One Islamic Institute and four Quranic schools	Equipment, furniture and 2 cars of Islamic Institute	Completed	Sept 1994 – May 1998	$305,000
	Irrigation			
F.S. of Kazandjik-Kizyl-Atrek irrigation canal	Feasibility study for the irrigation canal	Completed	Dec 1993 – Jun 2006	$263,219
Total			15 pcs.	$1,449,385,898

The IDB deals in Kyrgyzstan

Name	Summary	Status	Period	Size of investment
	Agriculture			
Preparation of a Feasibility Study for Halal Meat Processing Park	To prepare a F.S. for a Halal Meat Processing Park that assembles various components of the meat processing value chain — feedlot operations, veterinary services, slaughtering, cleaning processing, packaging — in the same location	Active	Apr 2019 — Jan 2020	$280,000
Reverse Linkage Between KYR and IND in Artificial Insemination Livestock	Reverse Linkage Between KYR and IND in Artificial Insemination Livestock	Active	Oct 2014 — Dec 2019	$300,000
Sustainable Villages Project	The project aims at reducing poverty in Jaiyal, Kemin and Panfilov Raions in Chui Province with the help of low-cost, sustainable and community-led interventions. The project will benefit app. 118,000 inhabitants in the areas of health, education, income and livelihood and agriculture. Special focus will be given to the poorer and the female segments of the community. It will adopt the approach of the Integrated Community Driven Development program	Active	Jun 2014 — Jan 2020	$9,110,200
Microfinance Project for Rural Development — OJSC «Kyrgyzstan Commercial Bank»	Of the 6 originally selected banks/MFIs, 3 banks/MFIs have been reallocated the approved funds. OJSC «Kyrgyzstan Commercial Bank» is one of the three. The main objective of the project is to alleviate poverty through providing access to financial resources to the impoverished communities within our LDMCs. The T. A. Grant is for the purpose of capacity building of the participating microfinance partners	Completed	Jun 2013 — Mar 2018	$1,075,310

Name	Summary	Status	Period	Size of investment
Microfinance Project for Rural Development — Center Kapital	The project aims at contributing and complementing the Government's efforts to achieve economic growth and alleviate poverty by providing and increasing the access of rural and urban poor, particularly women, to appropriate, reliable and affordable microfinance services. The project will also enhance existing microfinance schemes in reducing poverty and empowering the poor as well as introducing Shariah compliant microfinance products and services	Completed	Aug 2012 – Feb 2016	$1,177,848
Microfinance Project for Rural Development — Finance Partner	The Project aims at contributing and complementing the Government's efforts to achieve economic growth and alleviate poverty by providing and increasing the access of rural and urban poor, particularly women, to appropriate, reliable and affordable microfinance services. The Project will also enhance existing microfinance schemes in reducing poverty and empowering the poor as well as introducing Shariah compliant microfinance products and services	Completed	Aug 2012 – Mar 2018	$1,287,801
Project Preparation Facility for the ISFD Sustainable Villages Project	T.A. Grant is for reparation of a comprehensive baseline study for the IDB Sustainable Villages Project. The expected results of the study are: (i) Project site selection report, (ii) Project site reconnaissance report, (iii) Baseline and needs assessment report, (iv) Design of a project monitoring and information system	Active	Sep 2012 – Nov 2019	$94,273
Production of improved seeds of wheat (Jed. Decl.)	To support through Jeddah Declaration Phase II. LDMCs affected by the global crisis	Completed	Aug 2010 – Apr 2012	$400,000
Microfinance project for rural areas BAI ORDO Co.	The objective of the project is to support complement the government's efforts to achieve economic growth alleviate poverty by increasing the access of rural and urban poor, particularly women, to appropriate, reliable and affordable microfinance services	Completed	May 2010 – Jan 2013	$1,097,846

Name	Summary	Status	Period	Size of investment
Microfinance Project	The project aims at supporting and complementing the Government's efforts to achieve economic growth and alleviate poverty by increasing the access of rural and urban poor, particularly women, to appropriate, reliable and affordable microfinance services well as introduce Shariah complaint microfinance services and products	Completed	May 2010 — Feb 2016	$713,622
Replenishment of food security stocks- Phase I (Jed. Decl.)	The objective of the project is to replenishment of food security stocks to meet the urgent needs of the poor and vulnerable within the implementation of the short term of Jeddah Declaration	Completed	Dec 2008 — Apr 2011	$699,999
C.B. of International Charitable Foundation Project	The T.A. is to establish a microfinance umbrella organization and communication network, which will provide information on Microfinance best practices, training, institutional capacity building, marketing. The project will build up the capacity of the International Charitable Foundation (MEERIM) in the field of microfinance delivery, training, management and professional reporting and will increase access of the marginalized groups and the 'unbankables' to reliable and appropriate microfinance informationand services	Completed	Sep 2003 — Jan 2007	$130,000
	Water supply and irrigation			
Irrigated Agriculture Development in Issyk-Kul and Naryn Regions	Project development objective is to improve the livelihood of the rural population through sustainable agriculture development and water resources management with adaptation to climate change. The Project also aims to increase economic returns in the value chain for rural people through enhancing integration and market links	Active	Sep 2019 — Jan 2020	$19,797,120

Name	Summary	Status	Period	Size of investment
Rural Water Supply and Sanitation Improvement in Batken and Talas Regions	To assist the Kyrgyz Republic to (i) improve access and quality of water supply and sanitation services in target rural communities, (ii) strengthen capacity of institutions in the water supply and sanitation sector	Active	Apr 2019 — Jan 2020	$20,000,000
Validation Mission for the Reverse Linkage Sub-Project between Kyrgyz Republic (Recipient) and Egypt (Provider) on "Capacity Development on Water Resources Management"	Based on the outcomes of the validation mission, a Reverse Linkage sub-project may be formulated	Active	Jul 2018 — Jan 2020	$15,000
Diagnostic Mission for the Reverse Linkage Sub-Project between Kyrgyz Republic and Egypt on "Capacity Development on Water Resources Management"	The project aims at developing water supply system in Agadir and Chtouka Ait Baha areas. The project will benefit 1.565 mln inhabitants	Active	Apr 2018 — Oct 2019	$15,000

Name	Summary	Status	Period	Size of investment
Rural Water Supply and Sanitation Improvement Project	Project development objective is to assist the Kyrgyz Republic to (i) improve access and quality of water supply in target rural communities, (ii) improve sanitation services primarily in schools, and health centres in the selected villages and (iii) strengthen capacity of institutions in the water supply and sanitation sector	Active	Dec 2016 — Jan 2020	$20,048,504
Sarymsak Irrigation Scheme Development Project	The project aims at improving water supply on 1,685 ha irrigated land and developing additional 1,918 ha irrigated lands through upgrading Sarymsak irrigation system. The project will contribute in implementing the National Sustainable Development Strategy of the Government, which is aimed at improving the living conditions of the local communities, alleviating poverty, contributing to the national food security and enabling regional economic development	Active	Sep 2016 — Jan 2020	$13,196.540
Finance				
T.A. for Kyrgyzstan to Support Islamic Banking Framework	The objective of the T.A. is to provide to assist National Bank of Kyrgyz Republic in developing an appropriate regulatory, supervisory and Shariah governance frameworks for Islamic banking and Islamic monetary policy tools	Active	Jul 2018 — Jan 2020	$270,000
T.A. Grant for Feasibility Study to Establish an Islamic Bank in Kyrgyz Republic	Objective of the project is to provide a T.A. Grant for National Bank of Kyrgyz Republic to co-finance the expenses towards conducting a feasibility study for establishing an Islamic Bank in Kyrgyz Republic	Completed	Apr 2017 — Ict 2017	$49,590

Name	Summary	Status	Period	Size of investment
Development of Islamic Financial services industry	The objective of the project is to assist the Kyrgyz Rep. in implementation of the action plan of the government adopted by the decree of the president No. 146 dated 22 April 2008	Active	Jul 2012 — Oct 2019	$192,974
Introduction of Islamic Banking and Finance principles	The project aims to introduce Islamic Banking and Finance principles in Kyrgyzstan and to gradually convert Ecobank into an Islamic Bank by initially introducing Islamic Banking instruments and converting one of its full fledged branches to undertake Islamic based financing operations	Completed	Jan 2007 — Feb 2013	$255,000
Road construction				
Reconstruction of The North–South Alternative Highway Project (Balyktchy T — Jalal-Abad T)	The project aims at constructing a highway of 412 km linking the Northern and Southern regions of the country, of which 268 km need rehabilitation and 144 km need to be constructed. The section of the highway for reconstruction under this project is 50 km long (single carriageway, two lane national road), of which 24 km will be co-financed by IDB and SFD and 26 km section will be parallel financed by ADB	Active	Jun 2016 — Jan 2020	$12,262,775
Reconstruction of Osh–Batken–Isfana Road Project	The project will contribute to the reduction of transport costs and travel time along the Osh–Batken–Isfana road corridor; improve road safety planning; and repair and rehabilitate road infrastructure in and around Osh and Jalal Abad cities thereby creating temporary jobs. It involves reconstruction of 33 km part of the 360 km Osh-Isfana national road corridor	Active	Jun 2014 — Jan 2020	$21,332,330

Name	Summary	Status	Period	Size of investment
Reconstruction of Taraz-Talas-Suusamyr Road (Phase III) Project	The project aims at contributing the Government's Poverty Reduction Strategy Program to reduce poverty by ensuring access of the poor to basic social services including health, education and water as also economic infrastructure especially roads. The project will also promote regional integration between Kyrgyzstan and its neighbouring country Kazakhstan through reconstruction of 30 km long road section	Active	Apr 2013 — Jan 2020	$10,069,692
Reconstruction of Bishkek-Torugart Road Project	The project aims at providing year_round, reliable and direct land transport service between Bishkek and Kachi the nearest large city of China, which then links to Urumche and the rest of China. The project will also enhance trade and flow of passenger and freight traffic between Kyrgzstan and its neighbouring countries i.e. Kazakhstan and China	Completed	Aug 2010 — Apr 2018	$16,893,666
Taraz-Talas-Susamyr road (Phase II)	The objective is to reconstruct an existing road that will allow faster access to the border areas provide an important link with the neighbouring country of Kazakhstan	Completed	Aug 2008 — Feb 2013	$10,783,698
Reconstruc. of Osh-Irkeshtam road	The project aims to reconstruct road(44 km) between km 80+000 and km 124+000 which is severely damaged in order to fully accommodate the existing traffic as well as the forecasted traffic	Completed	May 2007 — Jan 2013	$13,842,838
Reconstruction of Taraz-Talas Suusamyr road	The proposed supplementary financing is vital to the achievement of the objective and original scope of the project to over the additional amount needed for the completion of the project	Completed	Apr 2003 — Jun 2011	$12,806,693
Construction of the Bishkek-Osh road	The project aims to construct two new sections of the Bishkek-Osh road at Madaniat detour (9 km length) and Jalalabad-Uzgen (40 km length) in order to bypass Uzbek territory and to provide this road with 100 km/hr design speed	Completed	Oct 1998 — Sep 2004	$9,809,010

Name	Summary	Status	Period	Size of investment
F.S. and detailed design for talas Jambul-Suusamyr road	To construct 150 km long 220 kv transmission line to provide elec. to 63,000 rural consumers including small industries commercial shops irrigation pumps and rural poor families	Completed	Nov 1997 — Dec 2009	$280,000
F.S. preparation of tender doc. for Bishkek-Torugart road	To prepare the techno-economic feasibility study, detailed design and the preparation of the tender documents for bishkek_torugart road that will connect the republic with neighbouring countries including IDB member countries	Completed	Nov 195 — Feb 1998	$306,640
Energy				
Central Asia-South Asia Electricity Transmission and Trade Project (CASA-1000)	The project aims at meeting the electricity demand in Afghanistan and Pakistan through the establishment of cross border energy exchange among 4 member countries as part of regional economic integration. The exchange will be utilizing efficient and environmentally friendly indigenous hydropower resources of Tajikistan and Kyrgyzstan. The project will provide sustainable, reliable and affordable electricity to Pakistan and Afghanistan while boosting foreign currency earning for Tajikistan and Kyrgyzstan through monetization of their seasonal surplus hydropower resources. It will include construction of 500 kV high voltage overhead transmission line connecting 4 countries	Active	Jan 2016 — Jan 2020	$46,197,513
Improvement of Electricity Supply in Arka Area of Batken Region	The project aims at construction of a new substation Razzakov, reconstruction of an existing substation Arka and construction of an overhead 51 km long 110 kV transmission line between them	Active	Jun 2014 — Jan 2020	$16,250,000

Name	Summary	Status	Period	Size of investment
Improvement of Electricity Supply in Bishkek and Osh Cities Project	The project aims at improving reliability and quality of electricity supply to Bishkek and Osh cities by upgrading the increasing substations. The project will result in (i) increased amount of electricity available to consumers, (ii) improved reliability and quality of electricity supply, and (iii) increased substations capacity in Bishkek by 40 and in Osh by 23.5 MVA.	Active	Sep 2011 — Jan 2020	$24,298,790
110 kV Aigultash to Samat transmission line substation	Construction of a single circuit 110 kV 140 kms long overhead transmission line from Aigultash to Samat	Completed	Jul 2007 — Jun 2013	$11,508,854
220 kV transmission line	To construct 150 km long 220 kV transmission line to provide elecricity to 63,000 rural consumers including small industries commercial shops irrigation pumps and rural poor families	Completed	Nov 1997 — Dec 2004	$9,375,663
Manufacture of distribution transformers substations	The project envisages the establishment of a new plant to manufacture 2,700 units of electric distribution transformers and 1,600 units of substations. The project would help utilize more effectively indigenous hydropower sources	Completed	Jun 1996 — May 2001	$8,000,000
Feasibility study for export of power		Completed	Nov 1993 — Dec 2009	$255,924
Education				
Improving Employability of Kyrgyzstani Youth	In view of high unemployment rate (25.3%), lack of socioeconomic adaptation skills for youth, and training institutions, particularly universities, are not preparing young people for jobs that are actually available, nor are they preparing them to create thier own opportunities through entrepreneureship training, the T.A. will improve the employability and livelihoods of youth by providing them with a range of critical skills	Completed	May 2014 — Jan 2016	$50,000

Name	Summary	Status	Period	Size of investment
One Islamic Institute and four Quranic schools	Construction of an Islamic institute and 4 Quranic schools	Completed	May 1995 — Jun 2001	$305,000
National language Arabic script programme	Printing of textbooks (Reallocated for Arabic Books for Islamic Center, Bishkek)	Completed	Jan 1994 — Jan 2003	$20,000
Emergency assistance to victims				
Emergency Assistance for the Affected People and Refugees in Kyrgyz Rep. and Uzbekistan	The main objective of the emergency assistance program is to contribute to the recovery of the general living conditions of the victims of Osh, Jalalabad and Bishkek affected in June 2010 ethnic riots between Kyrgyz and Uzbeks which resulted in the killing of hundreds of people and thousands of houses destroyed. It also caused a major refugee crisis across the border to Uzbekistan. The Turkish and the Qatar Red Crescent societies submitted a joint proposal for serving the returnees for (i) Construction of permanent housing and social facilities, and (ii) providing livelihoods (like livestocks and agricultural seeds)	Completed	Sep 2010 — Jun 2014	$1,000,000
Emergency assistance for the affected people and refugees	The Program aims to assist in providing livelihood support to the victims displaced by the unrest in the areas of Osh, Jalalabad and Bishkek and help them recover. The Program will focus on improving the economic and social conditions of the victims by creating the necessary physical and social environment in which both Kyrgyz and Uzbek communities can gain more easy access to common basic services and resources.	Completed	Jun 2010 — Jun 2014	$1,200,000

Name	Summary	Status	Period	Size of investment
	In June 2010, 4 days of ethnic rioting between Kyrgyz and Uzbeks, erupted in the southern city of Osh, putting the country in serious danger of fragmenting and resulted in the killing of hundreds and thousands of destroyed houses. It also touched off a major refugee crisis across the border to Uzbekistan. This project is in responseto the civil unrest that occurred in Kyrgyzstan in June 2010. The main objective of the assistance program is to contribute to the recovery of the general living conditions of the victims of unrest in the areas of Osh, Jalalabad and Bishkek. Most particularly, the assistance program is to focus on the improvement in the economic and social welfare of the victims by creating a necessary physical and social environment in which both Kyrgyz and Uzbek communities can gain access more easily			
Urgent Relief	Utilized for the construction and equipping of school in Osh	Completed	Sep 2003 — Mar 2005	$200,000
Assistance to earthquake victims of Toktogul region	Construction of schools and health centres	Completed	Jun 1993 — Jun 1998	$1,140,000
Public administration				
Strengthening the capacity of the Ministry of Finance	The objective of the project is to improve the management and coordination activity of the Ministry of Finance with regard to future and ongoing investment by enhancing its disbursement capacity, upgrading its IT infrastructure and providing adequate training for its specialists	Completed	Nov 2005 — Jun 2009	$249,951

Name	Summary	Status	Period	Size of investment
Capacity building for state property and direct investments (SPADI)	To enhance improve the product quality of the OREMI project through quality dev. int'l certification for the products. This will open new markets for the oremi products in the neighborhood countries, which will promote cooperation between IDB member countries through possible trade opportunities thr. export of transformers substations to these countries	Completed	Oct 2002 – Dec 2009	$174,000
Healthcare				
The national center of cardiology and therapeutics	Project provides for procurement of medical equipment and instruments required for diagnosis of heart conductive system such as ultrasound devices recording sensors cardiomonitors videobronchoscope system etc.	Completed	Nov 1997 – Jun 1999	$2,999,845
Specialized maternity hospital	To establish and equip a specialized maternity hospital with modern medical equipment and related facilities for applied research, diagnosis and treatment of women suffering from com complicated obsteric and gynecological diseases	Completed	Apr 1995 – Jul 1997	$1,984,635
Total		50 pcs.		$323,804,144

The IDB deals in Tajikistan

Name	Summary	Status	Period	Size of investment
Finance				
Global LoF to Tajikistan	Global LoF to Tajikistan Sector: Finance (Trade (Murabaha))	Active	Nov 2019 – Jan 2020	$7,800,000
Global Line of Finance Tajikistan	Global Line of Finance Tajikistan Sector: Finance (Trade (Murabaha))	Active	Jul 2019 – Jan 2020	$63,500
Agroinvest Bank	Agroinvest Bank Sector: Finance (Instalment Sale)	Active	Jun 2019 – Jan 2020	$136,000
Asr Leasing Company	Asr Leasing Company Sector: Finance (Equity)	Active	Dec 2017 – Mar 2018	$20,000,000
Asr Leasing Company	Asr Leasing Company Sector: Finance (Trade (Murabaha))	Active	Jun 2017 – Mar 2018	$1,000,000
T.A. to Develop Islamic Finance Sector (Phase-II)	For introduction and implementation of the Islamic banking principles in Tajikistan	Active	Dec 2015 – Jan 2020	$250,000
Microfinance Project for Rural Areas – National Bank of Tajikistan	The project aims at supporting and complementing the Government's efforts to achieve economic growth, alleviate poverty by increasing the access of rural and urban poor, particularly women, to appropriate, reliable and affordable microfinance services	Completed	May 2013 – Mar 2018	$6,208,366
Microfinance Project for Rural Areas – Tojiksodirotbonk, Tajikistan	The project aims at supporting and complementing the Government's efforts to achieve economic growth, alleviate poverty by increasing the access of rural and urban poor, particularly women, to appropriate, reliable and affordable microfinance services	Completed	Aug 2009 – Feb 2016	$1,549,272

Name	Summary	Status	Period	Size of investment
Microfinance Project for Rural Areas — Amonatbonk, Tajikistan	The Projects aims at supporting and complementing the Government's efforts to achieve economic growth and alleviating poverty by increasing the access of rural and urban poor, particularly women, to appropriate, reliable and affordable microfinance services. The project will also introduce Shariah compliant microfinance practices, services and products to the rural and semiurban poor	Completed	Aug 2009 — Feb 2016	$2,582,172
T.A. for Development of Islamic Banking	Capacity Building Assistance to Tajikistan Central Bank to set up legal; regulatory and supervisory framework for setting up Islamic Finance institutions	Completed	Nov 2011 — Nov 2015	$155,500
Microfinance Project	The project aims at contributing to the Government's efforts to achieve economic growth and poverty reduction, through supporting ongoing efforts to foster the microfinance industry via capacity building, and the provision of microfinancing to microentrepreneurs. The project will support the institutionalization of local MFIs, through providing additional sources of microfinance capital to service a larger number of clientele, and to built up their capacity to reach operational self sufficiency and longer term sustainability	Completed	Apr 2004 — Dec 2012	$679,547
F.S. for the establishment of an investment holding company	Development of Islamic Finance Enabling Environment	Completed	Dec 2003 — Aug 2008	$132,803
Capacity building of Amonatbank	—	Completed	May 2005 — Aug 2008	$252,913

Name	Summary	Status	Period	Size of investment
	Real Estate			
Savtechnik Intl (Saadi Tower)	Savtechnik Intl (Saadi Tower) Sector: Real Estate (Trade (Murabaha))	Active	Dec 2017 — Mar 2018	$25,000,000
Saadi Residential Dev. (Savtechnic)	Saadi Residential Dev. (Savtechnic) Sector: Finance (Leasing)	Active	Nov 2012 — Mar 2018	$5,000,000
Construction of hostel building	Construction of hostel and other facilities	Completed	Oct 1991 — Mar 1992	$200,000
	Education			
IsDB/GPE Project for Support to Implementation of the National Education Development Strategy of the Republic of Tajikistan	The project aims at: i) Enhancing access to quality education facilities in the selected districts; ii) Improving the efficacy of the Competency-Based Education (CBE) by reducing the gap between declared and implemented curriculum, supporting reform in assessment practices and stock-taking of various activities for effective implementation of CBE;and, iii) Supporting education sector policy, planning and evidence based resource allocation through strengthening of the EMIS and its piloting	Active	Dec 2019 — Jan 2020	$30,000,000
Transforming Care Work in the Rural Communities	The main objectives of this project are to reduce the total number of hours spent by women on unpaid care work and increase the number of hours women spend in income generating activities. Pilot Approach to Engage Women and Men in the Recognititon, Reduction and Redistribution of Unpaid Care Work	Active	Dec 2016 — Oct 2019	$100,000

Name	Summary	Status	Period	Size of investment
Vocational Literacy Program for Poverty Reduction Project (VOLIP)	The project aims at reducing poverty, particularly rural youth and women by enhancing access to education from the primary to the university level and help unskilled women workers access to job functional literacy, skills training and microfinance. The project will benefit 8,000 unemployed youth, 5,000 rural women workers and 244 trainers	Completed	Jan 2013 – Sep 2018	$9,977,964
Secondary Schools Development Project	The project aims at increasing access to improve quality of secondary education through construction and equipping of schools, training of teachers, curriculum development and capacity building. About 7,500 students and 336 teachers will benefit from the project	Completed	Apr 2012 – Sep 2017	$17,351,764
Construction of Imam Termizi University (Girls' section), Dushanbe	To complete the construction of Imam Termizi University (Girls' Section building). The building consists of classrooms, library, lecture hall and administration offices in the ground floor in addition to dormitories in the first floor	Completed	Jun 2008 – Jun 2008	$159,000
Reconstruction of secondary schools Phase II	The objective of Phase II of the project is to contribute to wards the improvement of the education sector through reconstruction of 7 secondary schools in 7 selected districts in Tajikistan in order to provide educational facilities for 4,546 students to pursue secondary education, facilitate direct employment for 1,000 teachers staff	Completed	Nov 2005 – Dec 2012	$10,326,716
Reconstruction and completion of secondary schools	The project is a part of the government's ambitious plans to reconstruct and complete about 168 schools. Total schools envisaged in this project are 23 of which 11 require rehabilitation and 12 for completion. The first phase of the project comprises the completion of 7 schools in the high density populated areas	Completed	Nov 1998 – Apr 2005	$9,437,400

Name	Summary	Status	Period	Size of investment
Institution & capacity building of the Ministry of Education	Printing of textbooks	Completed	Nov 1998 — Aug 2008	$229,706
Construction of 4 Quranic schools	Construction of Al Termezi University	Completed	Oct 1991 — Mar 2004	$100,000
Healthcare				
LLF- Improving Maternal, Neonatal and Child Health Services in Four Districts of Khatlon Region	The goal of the project is to help the Government realize the objectives of its National Health Strategy and to strengthen the health system with a view to improve maternal, newborn and child healthcare services in the Khatlon region. The specific project objectives are: i) Enhancing availability/ accessibility of Maternal, Neonatal, and Child Health services; ii) Institutional and human resources capacity building in the targeted health facilities; iii) Improving public awareness and health-seeking behavior; and, iv) Establishment of a functional referral system	Active	Aug 2019 — Jan 2020	$23,000,000
Dusti Pharmacy	Dusti Pharmacy Sector: Health (Trade (Murabaha))	Completed	Dec 2016 — Mar 2018	$13,152,000
Support to Prevention of Mother-to-Child HIV Transmission	The T.A. Grant is intended to prevent the transmission of HIV virus from mothers to their babies by enhancing the capacity of health workers and strengthening the monitoring and Evaluation system. It will also raise awareness of communities about the disease through promotion campaigns	Completed	Jun 2014 — Apr 2017	$398,585

Name	Status	Period	Size of investment
Construction and equipping of Dangara general hospital			
To provide adequate health services to the popul. of Khatlon region (oblast) and other neighboring regions. This will be accomplished through the construction of a new hospital and provision of modern medical equipment for the necessary medical services	Completed	Nov 2005 – Jun 2014	$1, 291,846
Emergency Surgical Care Center Project			
The Emergency Surgical Care Center (ESCC) is the only hospital of its kind in the country. The project aims at improving the provision of emergency surgical services by procuring of new medical equipment, that will help in providing advanced medical and surgical facilities to the patients in the greater Dushanbe area. The project will also provide an opportunity for the students in the Tajik State University to receive training on up to date medical equipment	Completed	Jan 2001 – Jan 2003	$2,489,190
Republican center for cardio- vascular thoracic surgery			
The project envisages the provision of equipment for rccts in order to requip the center with critically needed modern medical equipment. The new equipment will enable the center to conduct surgeries, treatment, research and higher education	Completed	Nov 1997 – Mar 1999	$2,927,384

Water supply and irrigation

Name	Status	Period	Size of investment
Improvement of Water Resources Management in Khatlon Region Project			
The Project development objective is to improve the livelihood of the rural population, through improvement of water resources management with resilience to climate change impacts. The project will result in increase of agriculture production by 110,000 tons per year; 2,000 new permanent, and 15,000 seasonal job opportunity will be created. 60,000 rural people will be provided with access to improved water supply	Active	Aug 2019 – Jan 2020	$15,000,000

Name	Summary	Status	Period	Size of investment
Dangara Valley Irrigation Network (Phase III) Project	The project aims at alleviating poverty in the project area by increasing the employment opportunities and household income of the target rural population through constructing 72 km of irrigation water pipe network and 66 km of drainage network to irrigate 1,750 ha of land in Dangara Valley	Active	May 2013 – Jan 2020	$26,554,720
Dangara Valley Irrigation Network Project (Phase II)	The project aims at alleviating poverty by increasing the household income of the rural population through contributing to increase the regional gross production of cotton and grain and generating employment for about 13,400 people in the agriculture and livestock sectors through the development of 1,750 ha of irrigated and in the Dangara Valley	Completed	Mar 2008 – Feb 2017	$15,796,537
Dushanbe Water Supply Project	The project aims at providing safe and reliable water supply services through reconstruction of two water treatment plants. It will contribute significantly to the improvement of the water quality and health conditions of the people. a population of 500,000 people will benefit from the project	Completed	May 2003 – Nov 2014	$11,783,800
Dangara Valley Irrigation Project	The project aims at improving the agricultural output and productivity through the development of 2,500 ha of irrigated land in the Dangara valley. The project includes: civil works, procurement and installation of equipment, supervision, training, etc.	Completed	Apr 2001 – Mar 2007	$8,007,390
Eng.design for irrigation of 6000ha in Dangara Valley	Developing a comprehensive bankable document and detailed engineering designs and tender documents for irrigation of 6000 ha in Dangara Valley in design packages of 2000 ha lots	Completed	Nov 1997 – Jun 2006	$280,000

Name	Summary	Status	Period	Size of investment
	Agriculture			
T.A. for Feasibility Study for Establishment of Fruit Cluster in Sugdh Province, Tajikistan	The overall objective of the project is to develop a fruit cluster in Sughd province with the state-of-art facilities for production and trade of dry fruits. The TA develop a comprehensive feasibility study for establishment of the fruit cluster in Sughd with a geographical concentration of producers and agro processors. The fruit cluster will help developing a competitive horticultural production and processing sector to promote Tajik value–added exports in compliance with international quality standards	Active	Dec 2017 — Jan 2020	$280,000
Petroleum, Wheat, Sugar	Petroleum, Wheat, Sugar Sector: Agriculture (Trade (Murabaha))	Completed	Feb 2016 — Mar 2018	$30,000,000
Petroleum, Wheat, Sugar	Petroleum, Wheat, Sugar Sector: Agriculture (Trade (Murabaha))	Completed	Dec 2014 — Mar 2018	$10,000,000
Agricultural Inputs	Agricultural Inputs Sector: Agriculture (Trade (Murabaha))	Completed	Feb 2008 — Mar 2018	$14,000,000
Production of improved seeds of wheat (Jed. Decl.)	To support through Jeddah Declaration Phase II. LDMCs affect ed by the global crisis	Completed	Jun 2010 — Feb 2012	$400,000
Replenishment of food security stocks–Phase I (Jed. Decl.)	The objective of the project is to replenishment of food security stocks to meet the urgent needs of the poor and vulnerable within the implementation of the short term of Jeddah Declaration	Completed	Nov 2008 — Apr 2011	$999,980

Name	Summary	Status	Period	Size of investment
Road construction				
Construction of Kulyab-Khalaikumb Road, Sections a and F (Kulyab-Shurobad and Shkev-Kalaikhumb)	The overall development objective of the project is to improve the living conditions of the population and to support the economic growth of the country by providing year-round, reliable and direct land transport service between the western part of Tajikistan, including the Capital Dushanbe, and the eastern Region of Gorno-Badakhshan. In addition, this project also aims at improving regional transit transportation and trade development with neighboring countries (Afghanistan, Uzbekistan, PRC, Pakistan, and Kyrgyz Republic)	Active	May 2017 — Jan 2020	$19,629,324
Shagon-Zigar Road (Phase III) Project	The project aims at providing year round, reliable and direct land transport services between the Western Tajikistan, including the capital Dushanbe, and the Eastern Region of Gorno-Badakhshan. It will reduce cost of transport and time. It will also enable enhanced trade and passenger traffic with neighbouring countries. The road will also link Tajikistan with the strategic Karakorum highway in China through Kulma Pass	Completed	May 2011 — Dec 2015	$19,001,500
Construction of Kulyab-Kalaikhum Road Project	The project aims at providing year round, reliable and direct land transport service between the Western part of Tajikistan, including the capital Dushanbe, and the Eastern Region of Gorno-Badakhshan. The project will also link Tajikistan with the strategic Karakorum highway in China through Kulma Pass, providing access to the sea port of Karachi, Pakistan, thus enhancing trade and flow of passenger and freight traffic between Tajikistan and its neighboring countries, Afghanistan, Kyrgyzstan, Uzbekistan and China	Completed	Jul 2009 — Oct 2018	$20,584,862

Name	Summary	Status	Period	Size of investment
Shagon–Zigar Road (Phase II) Project	The project is to provide year round, reliable and direct land transport service between the Western part of Tajikistan, and the Eastern Region of Gorno–Badakhshan, thus enhancing the territorial integrity of the country. The project will also link Tajikistan with the strategic Karakorum highway in China providing access to the deep sea port of Karachi, Pakistan, thus enhancing trade, flow of passenger and freight traffic between Tajikistan and its neighboring countries. The project will include: civil works for 9.75 km, construction supervision, etc.	Completed	Mar 2005 – Jan 2012	$13,365,299
Construction of Shagon–Zigar Road Project	The project aims at constructing Shagon–Zigar Road. The Shagon–Zigar Road, together with the Zigar–Shkev road, will provide reliable and direct access for East–West traffic between the Western parts of Tajikistan including the capital Dushanbe, and the Eastern region of Gorno–Badakhshan, thus enhancing the territorial integrity of the country. The project will also link Tajikistan to the first time with the strategic Karakorum highway in China through Kulma pass, providing access to the deep sea port of Karachi, Pakistan, thus enhancing trade and flow of passenger and freight traffic between Tajikistan and its neighboring countries Pakistan, Kyrgyz Republic, Uzbekistan and China. The project will include preparation of DED, Tender Documents, Civil Works, and Supervision	Completed	Mar 2001- Nov 2006	$9,063,600

Name	Summary	Status	Period	Size of investment
Construction of Murgab–Kulma pass highway	This project aims to provide continuous, reliable and direct land transport service between Murgab and Karakorum highway through Kulma pass. The wider objective of the project is to connect the Tajik national highway network with an int'l network via Karakorum highway in China and eventually to Pakistan, thus providing Tajikistan, a landlocked country	Completed	Nov 1999 – Jan 2005	$9,309,672
F.S. for construction of road Shagon–Zigar	The objective of the project to carry out a techno–economic feasibility study for 30.7 km Shagon–Zigar road in South–East of Dushanmbe	Completed	Nov 1998 – Feb 2005	$258,274
F.S. for constructing 15kms road from Kulma pass to Karakorum	Conducting a techno–economic feasibility study, detailed design for constructing 15 kms of road from Kulma pass to Karakorum highway	Completed	Nov 1997 – Jun 2006	$280,000
Public administration				
C.B. of the State Committee on Investment and State Property	The project aims at capacity building of the State Committee on Investment and State Property Management.	Completed	May 2013 – Aug 2016	$250,000
Familiarization Visit for 5 Officials from the IDB, Office of the President	The main objectives of this project are to reduce the total number of hours spent by women on unpaid care work and increase the number of hours women spend in income generating activities	Completed	Feb 2017 – Jun 2017	$18,000

Name	Summary	Status	Period	Size of investment
Technical Assistance for Capacity Building of the Ministry of Energy and Water Resources	The main objective of the Technical Assistance is to support the enhancement of work environment in the newly established Ministry of Energy and Water Resources by assisting in building an up-to-date information management system and enable the Ministry to improve its legislation for Renewable Energy and Energy Efficiency	Active	Jan 2017 – Jan 2020	$281,294
C.B. of the Ministry of Economy and Trade Project	The project aims at improving the management and coordination activity of the Ministry of Economy and Trade in dealing with privatization, private sector investment and small and medium enterprises (SMEs). The project aims to procure modern IT equipment, create a database and software with investment and private sector related information, conduct study on the problems of current privatization process, develop framework to help the SMEs and enhance the human resources of the MET through training	Completed	Sep 2003 – Feb 2010	$216,785
Organization of International Investment Conference in Tajikistan and Uzbekistan	The T.A. will strengthen economic ties and transfer of human and monetary capital between OIC countries and CIS countries. The T.A. will provide the opportunity for OIC businessmen to network and establish business relations with their counterparts in Tajikistan and Uzbekistan. It will cover air travel cost; hotel accommodations and logistics; conference and audio-visual facilities; and other related expenditures	Completed	Mar 2003 – May 2006	$324,000

Name	Summary	Status	Period	Size of investment
Capacity Building of National Bank of Tajikistan Project	The T.A. is for building and improving the country's institutional capacity to reform the banking sector particularly enhancing the human resources of NBT in formulating and implementing sound macroeconomic and financial policies. The main thrust is to provide capacity building and support for training in critical areas of banking that will improve among other things, the role of NBT, as a central bank, in regulatory and bank supervision matters; management systems, and provide assistance in privatization of medium and large enterprises, and assistance in private sector development. The project will enable NBT to conduct tailor made programs for its employees as well as those from the commercial banks in Tajikistan. The T.A. will cover procurement of office equipment and software and support for NBT to conduct in-house training courses for bank employees	Completed	Sep 2001 – Jun 2007	$237,000
	Energy			
Reconstruction of Ravshan Electricity Substation Project	The project aims at promoting economic growth and improving the living standards in the Tursunzade city and Shahrinav regions through supplying reliable electricity. The project would provide a huge support to agricultural growth and setting up of small industries in these two regions and thus contribute to poverty reduction	Active	Feb 2014 – Nov 2019	$12,990,094
Regional power transmission interconnection project	The project aims to construct power transmission line for selling access power (300 mW) to Afghanistan. The line will be from Sangtuda to Kunduz	Completed	Oct 2007 – Jul 2013	$14,544,999

Name	Summary	Status	Period	Size of investment
Mini Hydropower Plants in the Rural Areas Project	The project is to provide a reliable supply of electricity in rural areas of Tajikistan where supply is limited during summer, and, especially, winter periods owing to a combination of generating capacity problems during peak periods of demand, energy availability constraints and transmission system supply constraints. This objective will be realized through the construction of 8 (eight) mini hydropower plants in rural areas of Tajikistan located North and East of Dushanbe	Completed	Apr 2004 – May 2013	$11,967,490
Power Project	The project aims at improve quality of life of the people and supporting pro_poor economic growth through increased availability of electric power and assist in the post_conflict economic recovery of Tajikistan. The objective of IDB funded Part «С» is tosecure reliable supply of power to the capital Dushanbe (population around 750,000) and the surrounding areas. The planned refurbishment will significantly reduce the energy shortage in Dushanbe and the electrical losses in the transformers. The Project will involve upgrading of distribution facilities in Dushanbe, rehabilitating the Nurek hydropower station, rehabilitation and reinforcement of power transmission and distribution facilities in war damaged areas, and provision of assistance for strengthening of operational and management capabilities of Barki Tojik	Completed	Jan 2001 – Feb 2011	$19,257,456
F.S of hydropower plants in rural areas	The objective of the project is to carry out F.S. for the construction of small hydropower plants located in the rural areas of Tajikistan	Completed	Jan 2001 – Apr 2006	$248,000

185

Name	Summary	Status	Period	Size of investment
	Emergency assistant to victims			
Emergency relief assistance to victims of flood	Emergency assistance through Tajikistan Red Crescent	Completed	May 2010 — Feb 2011	$200,000
Emergency aid to victims of the severe weather, 2008, in Tajikistan	To Purchase and distribute medicine, blankets, tents, winter clothes & food items to the people	Completed	Mar 2008 — Jan 2016	$200,000
Total		64 pcs.		$488,281,704

Source: complied according to the Islamic Development Bank[1].

---

[1] https://www.isdb.org/projects/data

APPENDIX D

Cognitive map of the respondents' perceptions of Islamic Finance in Russia

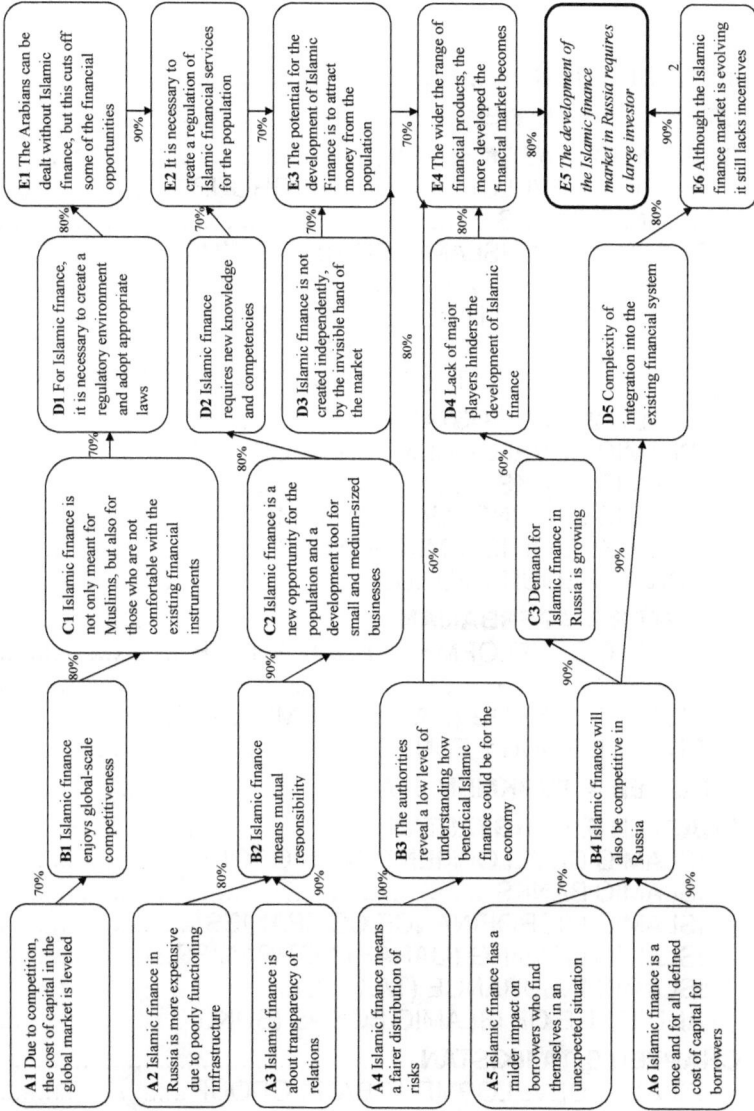

A1 Due to competition, the cost of capital in the global market is leveled

A2 Islamic finance in Russia is more expensive due to poorly functioning infrastructure

A3 Islamic finance is about transparency of relations

A4 Islamic finance means a fairer distribution of risks

A5 Islamic finance has a milder impact on borrowers who find themselves in an unexpected situation

A6 Islamic finance is a once and for all defined cost of capital for borrowers

B1 Islamic finance enjoys global-scale competitiveness

B2 Islamic finance means mutual responsibility

B3 The authorities reveal a low level of understanding how beneficial Islamic finance could be for the economy

B4 Islamic finance will also be competitive in Russia

C1 Islamic finance is not only meant for Muslims, but also for those who are not comfortable with the existing financial instruments

C2 Islamic finance is a new opportunity for the population and a development tool for small and medium-sized businesses

C3 Demand for Islamic finance in Russia is growing

D1 For Islamic finance, it is necessary to create a regulatory environment and adopt appropriate laws

D2 Islamic finance requires new knowledge and competencies

D3 Islamic finance is not created independently, by the invisible hand of the market

D4 Lack of major players hinders the development of Islamic finance

D5 Complexity of integration into the existing financial system

E1 The Arabians can be dealt without Islamic finance, but this cuts off some of the financial opportunities

E2 It is necessary to create a regulation of Islamic financial services for the population

E3 The potential for the development of Islamic Finance is to attract money from the population

E4 The wider the range of financial products, the more developed the financial market becomes

E5 The development of the Islamic finance market in Russia requires a large investor

E6 Although the Islamic finance market is evolving it still lacks incentives

70% 80% 90% 100% 60% 70% 80% 90% 70% 80% 70% 80% 60% 90% 80% 2

CONTENTS